20@60

Transamerica run from Jacksonville Beach to San Diego

20@60

A Baby Boomer's Run Across The U.S.

By
Richard Cohen

20@60

A Baby Boomer's Run Across The U.S.©

Cover art by www.KillerGraffix.com

Editing, Composition, and Typography by www.ProEditingService.com

ISBN-13: 978-1484017739

ISBN-10: 1484017730

Published by Digital Lightbridge
11902 Little Road
New Port Richey, Florida 34654
www.DigitalLightbridge.com

Dedication

To my wife, Sheryl

To my beautiful children
Jason, Jeffrey, Julie, Danielle, Rachel and Ari

In memory of my mother and father.
They would have gotten a kick out of this—when the initial shock wore off.

Ted and Miriam Deutsch
What a family means.

Table of Contents

Prefix IV.   *Foreword*

Prefix V.   *Preface*

Prefix VI.   *About the Author*

Prefix VII.   *Acknowledgments*

Prefix VIII.   *Introduction*

Chapter 1.   *A Much Needed Break* 1

Chapter 2.   *An Abbreviated Training Period* 5

Chapter 3.   *Getting the Word Out* 15

Chapter 4.   *Telling Our Son* 19

Chapter 5.   *Change* 21

Chapter 6.   *The Run Begins* 27

Chapter 7.   *My Evolving Daily Routine* 29

Chapter 8.   *My Mirror Image* 31

Chapter 9.   *A Question of Balance* 33

Chapter 10.   *May I Pray with You?* 40

Chapter 11.   *Coping Skills—The Bridges* 42

Chapter 12.   *Food—Eat, Drink and be Happy* 50

Chapter 13.   *The Eight States* 89

Chapter 14.   *The 272* 91

Chapter 15.   *A Special Appreciation: The Jewish Connection* 102

Chapter 16.   *Why?* *106*

Chapter 17.   *Singing in the Rain—Porn Shop Stop* *112*

Chapter 18.   *A Random Act of Kindness* *114*

Chapter 19.   *The Cancer Biker* *116*

Chapter 20.   *Reconnecting After 43 Years* *119*

Chapter 21.   *Texas* *123*

Chapter 22.   *Inspiration on I-10 to California* *126*

Chapter 23.   *Mother's Day—The Café; Buffalo Gap, Texas* *128*

Chapter 24.   *A Few Noteworthy Events* *131*

Chapter 25.   *Indian School Road Disaster* *166*

Chapter 26.   *Billy the Kid and Historic Route 66* *169*

Chapter 27.   *Alien Nation—Roswell, New Mexico* *173*

Chapter 28.   *The Return of the Sheriff* *175*

Chapter 29.   *Taiban, Yeso and Glamis* *177*

Chapter 30.   *VLA—Very Large Array* *180*

Chapter 31.   *Fire and Smoke* *182*

Chapter 32.   *I-10 State Trooper—Not Cool!* *187*

Chapter 33.   *Phoenix and Scottsdale* *190*

Chapter 34.   *The Wigwam Resort—Oasis in the Desert* *195*

Chapter 35.   *Dips in the Road—Southern California* *197*

Chapter 36.   *The Little Lady* *200*

Chapter 37.   *Splashdown in the Pacific* *204*

Chapter 38.   *The End of the Road* *210*

Conclusion.   *Comments from Friends and Strangers* *213*

               Addendum *221*

Foreword

Penned by an exceptional, very dedicated runner, what follows is one person's prescription regarding how to find and follow a path towards self-fulfillment. Whether or not you are a runner, should you discover that the following quote resonates within, I would encourage your further investigation of this author's captivating journey.

"When was the last time that you sat back, alone, and questioned what you were really doing and how content you were?"

Those questions are amongst the existential issues addressed via this intimate, entertaining autobiographical account of the author's run across America: Why am I here? What am I doing about it? Am I happy and comfortable with those answers? This book provides a simple, practical, yet powerful "How-to" manual about personal transformation.

Within these pages, the author shares his own brand of psychological alchemy, a process that has provided him with both purpose and hope where once but doubt and fear resided. Step after step, as the miles accumulate, the reader is invited to share the runner's evolving mindset. His worldview emphasizes the indefatigable power of the individual as the very personal solution to the global economic and geopolitical problems that currently plague our planet. Daily, we are assaulted by the media with news of doom and gloom and, without some means of combating the feelings that we are but helpless victims, hope and belief in oneself are becoming the exception rather than the rule.

However, there are those who dare persevere by embracing those personal traits that, collectively, have made this a great country. It is for these courageous individuals, those who are desirous of having a "hand in" resolving our ubiquitous ills, rather than those content with receiving a "handout," for whom this book was written. Herein lies a road map to assist in one's daily quest towards action, and personal gratification. With each page, the reader is reminded that "the longest journey starts with but one step." (Lao-Tzu and Lionel Giles, *The Sayings of Lao-Tzu*, 1904, 51)

Bill Gotthelf, Ph.D.
Psychologist

Preface

I am not a writer, nor will I consider myself a writer after this book is published. I am an observer of people's behavior and an appraiser of my own. I have enjoyed going through changes in my life and observing the positive results of those changes. I have learned through my miles of running that life is beautiful and fun, and an amazing experience to be internalized for personal pleasure and contentment. Mostly, I have learned to appreciate what I have and not be concerned with what I have lost or never had.

Running has afforded me the opportunity to learn to see life from different angles—to walk around situations, scratch my head, and then decide which view is most reasonable and closest to an unfiltered reality. I learned to view life from different vantage points. My tunnel vision and single lens through which I narrowly viewed the world in former years have been transformed into a 3D IMAX screen where I can see the world with much more clarity and pleasure.

I want to experience my share of enjoyment and pleasure during my split second in life, and have no regrets when I close my eyes for the final time.

This book is about a running journey across our country. I experienced my run as simply a 5½-month tour through the parts of America many bypass and forget. It addresses and highlights only a small fraction of my experiences and the sheer pleasure I was afforded along the way. The beauty, peace, and solitude—and the occasions of total silence of nature—were breathtaking. The brief escape from the rigors of everyday life and technology was priceless.

This book was started in August 2011, as Sheryl and I were staying in Magnolia Springs, Alabama. I wanted my children and grandchildren to know more of the details about my run. I was concerned that as time passed, I would begin to forget. I wanted to have a written account so when I became senile and started to drool I could have a journal to refer to. What started as a brief journal for them became a book.

For 600 running hours, I experienced life as it should be lived. I am one lucky guy.

Richard Cohen

VI

About the Author

In 1989, Richard began to train for and run marathons: the Marine Corps marathon twice, the New York Marathon twice, the Chicago Marathon, the Twin Cities Marathon, and the 100th running of the Boston Marathon.

In 2011, Richard became only the 128th individual in the previous 102 years, since 1909, to make a running journey crossing of the United States.

Richard grew up in Montgomery, Alabama, where his love for running and pole vaulting began in school. Graduated from the University of Alabama with a bachelor's degree in psychology, he received his master's degree in counseling psychology from the University of Massachusetts in Boston.

RICHARD COHEN DURING HIS CROSS-COUNTRY TREK.

Richard worked for the Framingham Counseling Center where he counseled young adults and families.

Richard has owned both manufacturing and retail businesses for over 37 years as well as serving as a consultant and board member in the bedding industry.

Richard has been married to Sheryl for more than 40 years. They have three children: Jason, Jeffrey, and Julie; daughter-in-law Danielle; and grandchildren Rachel and Ari.

Richard and Sheryl presently reside in Florida where there are plenty of parks, beaches, and sunshine.

Ⓥ️Ⅱ
Acknowledgments

First and foremost, I want to thank my wife, Sheryl, for the enthusiasm she put into supporting me every day of the run: buying my food and drink, finding motels and making reservations, dropping me off and picking me up every day—119 trips to and from drop off points, sometimes 300 miles in a day—just so I could run 20. Thank you to my best friend of 42 years with whom I laughed, who was my nurse when I was hurt, and who made my run a dream come true.

To my children, Jason, Jeffrey, Julie, Danielle, Rachel, and Ari: Thank you for your help and enthusiastic support before and during the run. Thank you, Jason and Rachel, for surprising me and being with me as I touched the Pacific. Thank you, Julie, for serving as my motivation—to give you that hug in the Pacific Ocean. And to Jeffrey, thank you for being my "go-to" guy, the one who broke the news about my crazy idea to run across the country. Thank you, Danielle, for your invaluable creative help and input as I wrote this book.

To my brother-in-law, Nessim, sister-in-law Diane, and sister-in-law Suzie: Thank you for your total support and concern for me every day of my run. Nessim and Diane, your being at the end to help me celebrate and, Suzie, your plans to come from day one meant more to me than you can imagine. Your sincere concern and support showed in what you did and not just what you said.

To my sister, Ellen, and my two brothers, Mark and Marshall, thank you for your interest, support, and concern.

To my cousins Brian and Susan, thank you for your invaluable help and friendship during the final weeks of the run and for being such helpful and gracious hosts during our stay in San Diego after the run.

To Katherine, thank you for building the Web site to get us going on the run, and for all the technical help with the geeky Internet stuff. We can't thank you enough for taking care of our house.

To Alan, Mary, and Dickie, childhood friends who supported me in every way possible. I couldn't ask for better friends.

To Paulette Bethel, thank you for your professional editing and writing advice and for your patience during the process. I couldn't have found a better advisor.

To my good friend Bill Gotthelf for allowing me to pick your brain about the brain.

To Avi Levine of NefeshB'Nefesh, a Jewish charity in Israel, for creating our final website and helping to get my blog started.

Thank you to all who contributed to my run, to the United Way, to NefeshB'Nefesh, and to friends and total strangers from all over the world who wrote and called to lend support and encouragement.

Introduction

....

I'm going to run across the United States.

It was that simple. That thought was so strong, so definitive, and so liberating an idea that, as soon as I thought it, I knew it was supposed to happen, was going to happen.

The same feeling overcame me in eighth grade when I decided to learn how to pole vault, at age 38 when I decided to run a marathon, and again at age 40 when I decided to go to graduate school. I can sense when a flash thought should be acted upon, regardless of its position in left field.

At first, I thought it would be a 4000-mile run. For some reason, I erroneously thought the width of the United States was about that. I was surprised to find in my MapQuest search, that it was actually about 2350 miles; a southern route from Jacksonville, Florida, to San Diego, California—from the Atlantic to the Pacific Ocean. The miles were approximate since the MapQuest mileage was based on route I-10 and I would be running on U.S., state, and county roads. The starting and ending points were fixed and finite—the right-hand ocean to the left-hand ocean.

That's what I was going to do. I turned 60 in September 2010, so this was a belated birthday gift from me, to me.

Since I had run seven marathons, I immediately decided that 20 miles a day would be a good daily distance. Overnight recovery after each day's run was realistic and it would take only about 120 running days. I was excited to do this, but I didn't want to celebrate my 70th birthday on the road.

I had to allow for a few personal days off in anticipation of my father's passing away, my granddaughter's birthday, and my niece's wedding. I added a few injury days or just rest days as a margin for error. Out of respect for my son's religious convictions of keeping the Sabbath, I decided not to run on Saturdays. As it turned out, I was off by only one day. The trip took 118 days, plus a final morning of 2.3 miles for the local news stations; thus 119 days. This was an off-the-cuff calculation that turned out to be fairly accurate.

The timing was perfect. My wife, Sheryl, and I had just closed our business, a baby furniture and accessory store in Norcross, Georgia. The poor economy made it impossible for us to keep the doors open any longer. Our 12 years in this business came to an end on October 21, 2010, just 10 days after my mother passed away. I knew the time had come to close when my landlord called me as I was leaving the cemetery grounds, screaming at me to send the rent check. We loved our business, but we had exhausted all of our financial resources, as well as being physically and emotionally spent. We had worked almost 7 days a week for the prior 2½ years, trying to keep the business alive.

Although I'm 60 years old, I don't feel, act, or think like I imagine a 60-year-old is supposed to feel, act, and think. Looking back, I see my dad acting 70 when he was 50. That was not my idea of the process of getting older. I have always felt that my experiences, learning from my mistakes and my running, would overcome most aging factors.

I told my older son, Jason, when he was 12 and I was 36, that a very positive attitude can overcome a lot of shortcomings. This conversation occurred when we were playing tennis together. I told Jason, who went on to become a Massachusetts tennis scholar athlete, that I could beat him despite his talent and years of lessons and the fact that I hadn't played tennis in over ten years. It was all in the mind, I said.

He beat the crap out of me—6-1, 6-1, and I learned a very important lesson. A positive attitude goes only so far when a particular skill is needed to compete. That beating on the court was a red letter day for my son. Despite the score, I won. I got to experience my son's joy and rise in confidence. Actually, we both won and walked off the tennis court laughing. Sheryl, an observer of this "lesson," couldn't have been happier with the outcome.

I am fortunate that I chose a sport for which I am a natural. In high school, I was a sprinter and pole vaulter, so running was something I always loved—short runs, that is. Anything over a 220-yard dash I considered a distance run. My first mile ever was in the Alabama state decathlon championship in 1968. I couldn't believe I had to actually run four times around the track. But as I got older, I began to gravitate toward distance. I also began to realize the benefits, both physical and psychological, in distance running.

Again, I found the key was attitude. I had always felt that running was simply a time to think and dream while I just happened to be moving. When I finally "got it," with respect to the pleasures of running, the miles began to fly by. After my run across the United States, I figured that I had run over 7500 miles between 1989 and 2011. That was quite a bit of thinking, dreaming, self-reflection, philosophizing, and perspective changing, and simply feeling good and content. Although I do wear a watch when I run, I rarely check it. I never listen to music. It disrupts my thoughts.

When I was training for marathons in my 40s, I had a simple routine. I'd begin training at the end of March, when the weather in Boston was just beginning to warm a bit. I'd run until I was able to run 10.2 miles in 75 minutes. I had a route through Framingham and Sudbury, which was 5.1 miles, and then the return run. Once I was running seven-and-a-half minute miles for 10 miles, I felt I was ready to begin my real training, usually around July, for a fall marathon. I had a very simple, easy training schedule. I'd run six miles Wednesday evening after work. On Saturdays, I'd run my

10.2 miles, and on Sundays, I'd run my long distances—12, 14, 15, 16, 18, 20. What happened to the 13, 17 and 19 miles? I do not know. Then I'd run 18, 16, 15, 14, 12 on the backside of the training as I approached the date of the marathon.

The Saturday before the week of a marathon, I'd run my final long run—15 miles. I'd start at my house and run to downtown Framingham—to the train station—and back.

The Wednesday evening before Sheryl and I were to leave for the marathon, I'd run around our street three times, a three-mile run; I considered it my victory lap. I'd end in front of my house and raise my arms like Rocky Balboa in the movie *Rocky*. It was another victory over pain, poor conditions, rude drivers, and the chance of injury—the training process complete.

To me, it was the end of the process, a very satisfying, exhilarating six months that I loved. It was the process of training that I loved: the runs, the solitude, and the satisfaction of doing something that was extremely healthy and gratifying, not to mention the compounding of psychological strength I derived with each marathon experience.

The marathon itself was the icing on the cake. It was the reward for the months of training. I never saw the actual marathon as the ultimate goal. It was simply the "final run" of the process. This was where I experienced the pain and joy all wrapped up in one final run of the year before winter set in. It was the process of "getting to" an end result that I embraced, not just the end itself. If not, the point of the journey is totally missed. How miserable it must be for a runner to train only because it is necessary to complete a marathon. What a waste of the joy of training. If you can't enjoy the process while getting to the end, it is an exercise in misery until the ultimate goal is reached— if it is reached.

I planned to run across the United States. If I couldn't look forward to the daily 20-mile runs, and only looked ahead to the anticipated few moments of joy as I put my foot into the Pacific Ocean, I would never have made it past Jacksonville.

Sheryl and I loved the marathon weekends. We always made it a four-day event. We'd fly or drive to the city of the marathon on a Friday, go to the marathon headquarters on Saturday to get my number and running package and check out the runner's fair. This is where booths were set up to sell running gear. I always bought a long sleeve T-shirt at the fair, as a reminder of the event. As it turned out, when I ran across the country, it was these seven long sleeve T-shirts that I wore every day of my run. They are tattered and thread-bare now but still hanging around as reminders of each marathon and my ultimate marathon; the 119-day run.

I have lost interest in keeping, or even purchasing things now, but when it comes to my running "stuff," I keep what helped change me and makes me a very content person.

Saturday night, before each Sunday's marathon, we'd bypass the traditional group pasta dinner put on by the marathon sponsors and, instead, go to a small Italian restaurant for our own private carb load. I'd have the same dinner each time, a big plate of spaghetti and tomato sauce, salad, a lot of bread, and water; nothing fancy, just basic high carb dining.

Sunday was the race and I always spent the afternoon after finishing in glorious pain. That evening we'd go out for a celebratory dinner—I would walk slowly, was very stiff, and usually had a mild headache.

Monday we relaxed and then flew or drove home in the afternoon. It was always a great weekend for both of us.

People have asked me why I chose 20 miles to run every day.

"Why not just run a marathon—IT'S ONLY SIX MORE MILES!"

The reason I chose 20 miles is that I could recover overnight and be fresh to run the next day. I had realized that the last four or five miles, for me, were what the marathon was all about. Also, if you read about marathon training and running, you will find that it is general knowledge that at or around the 20-mile mark, you "hit the wall." This is the point at which your body begins to break down. Carbs are depleted, electrolytes are low, and your mental and physical health begins to deteriorate. This is exactly what happened to me. I didn't know too much about the conventional wisdom of running a marathon. I just did what felt right for me, and it seemed to work.

I was always fine for the first 21 to 22 miles. After that I always felt that my mind was dragging a dead hunk of meat toward the finish line. I found that I couldn't focus on any one thought, and my body was in excruciating pain. It would take me approximately 2 hours and 45 minutes to run 20 miles. It took anywhere from an hour and 15 minutes to an hour and a half to run the final 6.2 miles! My pace slowed and my only mission, at that point, was to finish. I now realize that if I trained harder and more efficiently for those last six miles, I'd have minimized the pain and suffering.

But my mission was not to beat a time, or place in the top 20 percent of the field. My No.1 goal was simply to complete the marathon—and enjoy the weekend experience.

Fortunately, I learned very early on in my training that the key to finishing a marathon is to get so deeply entrenched in my mind that nothing would prevent me from finishing; that's simply the way it was. The desire and need to finish is greater than the relief of stopping. My whole mental state was that there was no option except finishing. No stopping, no resting, no nothing—except crossing that finish line.

That concept is what allowed me to run and finish seven marathons—and to run across the country. This was not a brief thought. It became an integral part of me, and I knew that unless I was seriously injured I would finish the marathon.

I was very fortunate that I ran those many miles virtually injury free. But, in the event of an injury, I would have crawled across the finish line—or into the Pacific. It became a frame of mind that gave me no wiggle room to quit; quitting was never an option. It worked for me.

I was not a fast marathoner. I had always considered myself a "casual marathoner." By that I mean that my time was never an issue or a goal. My goal in running the marathon was to finish, and enjoy the 26.2-mile run. I saw my marathons as a tour of the city in which I was running. I was always taking in the sights as I ran the route. My times ranged from 3:54 in Chicago to 4:30 in Boston. I wanted my runs to be fun. I never stopped or walked during my runs. I put absolutely no pressure on myself to finish in a prescribed time. I set no pre-race time goals. This exercise in training and running marathons was fun for me. I was not going to turn it into an obsessive work project.

A neighbor in Framingham, a marathoner himself, told me that running a marathon would change one's life. I learned the truth to that as I stepped across my first finish line at the 1989 Marine Corps Marathon in Washington, D.C.

My younger brother, Marshall, and I ran together. He had run two previous marathons and was excited to run another with me. As we approached the finish line around the back of the Iwo Jima Memorial, we clasped hands and, raising our arms above our heads in triumph, crossed the finish line together. I won't go into the details of that first marathon experience because the only thing that mattered was how I felt and reacted after we completed the race.

After we finished, I stopped and walked a few steps away from my brother. A marine came up to me and put a finisher's medal around my neck. He shook my hand and said, "Congratulations, great job." As he walked away, I put my hands on my knees, lowered my head, and cried. It was a very quiet, brief, but powerful release with tears running down my face. A few seconds later, I put my hands over my face, wiped my eyes, stood up, and it was over.

The physical pain I was feeling was excruciating. My body was vibrating from the pounding of over four hours and 12 minutes: 45,000 steps. As I stood there, I felt this black cloud of self-doubt leave my body. I'm speaking metaphorically but the experience was real. In the throes of this extreme physical pain, I felt an instantaneous change come over me; like nothing I had ever experienced before. This sudden change startled me. I was so proud of what I had just accomplished. A sprinter afraid of anything more than 220 yards had just run 26.2 miles.

In an instant, my view of myself was transformed into something positive and good and filled with much more confidence. I was on top of the world.

I found a spot and lay down on the ground while my brother got us some butter cookies and orange juice. Cookies and juice never tasted so good. Every bone and muscle in my body was stiff and sore. It was the greatest feeling in the world. I've never felt so bad and so good at the same time. It did, in fact, change my life.

So, my marathoning ended as I crossed the finish line at Copley Square in Boston; seven. I decided that the 100th running of the Boston Marathon was a fitting end to my marathon career. I had experienced great trips, great runs, and great memories. I started out wanting to run just one marathon to see what it was all about. Seven marathons and five cities later, I got the message.

Though I no longer run marathons, I have never stopped running. Whenever we go out of town, I run. I run for no less than an hour, about six miles. That distance and time allows for a good workout with plenty of time to think and dream. I don't run every day, and sometimes not for months, but it always returns—the desire for solitude and sweating and simply feeling good.

A Much Needed Break

When we walked out of our retail store for the final time, in October 2010, Sheryl and I were sad. We had put our hearts and souls into our business. But, as I taped the message of closing on the front door, I also felt a strong sense of relief. The last two years had been tough trying to keep the business going as the economy slipped deeper and deeper into a recession.

The media described the economic downturn of 2008 as a recession. I had been through many recessions. This was no recession; it was more a recession/depression. We had put all our financial resources into the business. We had tried our best to survive but the well was dry.

We took a week off and then I started looking online for employment possibilities. The more I looked, the more I looked realistically at my situation. I was a 60-year-old entrepreneur with 37 years' experience in both manufacturing and retail. I had a B.S. in Psychology and an M.Ed. in Counseling Psychology. I noticed jobs available in many different areas—none even remotely matching my entrepreneurial skill. Plus, I began to wonder if I would even make a suitable employee. I checked out small business consulting. As I sat and scanned the possibilities, I came to one conclusion: I wasn't really ready or even interested in getting back to work. I was burned out; I needed a break.

It wouldn't be a permanent break. We couldn't afford that. But I needed a temporary break from what I'd done for the past 37 years. I sat back in my chair, looked at my computer screen, and said to myself, "I can't do this now; I can't just get back into the same routine, even if I can find a job." My heart wasn't into it anymore. I really needed to take a step back and look at my place in life. I had just turned 60 years old and we'd had a great run leading up to this stage of our lives. Our kids were all doing well and it was just the two of us that we had to be concerned with. I felt like I was physically and psychologically whipped from trying to keep our business afloat. I genuinely left it all on the field: my money, my heart, my soul, my energy, my motivation. As I sat there, I felt I needed to do something for myself and Sheryl; for ourselves—not for the kids, not out of any responsibility or obligations, or duty. Something just for the two of us—a break.

As bad as things were, the bright spot was that for the first time as an adult I was able to take a step back, remove myself from my daily routine and realistically look at my life, my prospects and, more importantly, ask myself what I wanted out of life at this stage, and in the future. Once I let go of the notion that I had to hang on to my former lifestyle, income level, and place of residence, I was open and free to let go of the comfort of familiarity and embrace new possibilities.

Do I want to keep working forever? Do I want to continue the grind, in a very unfriendly, almost hostile business climate? Do I want to continue the same morning routine and evening routine? What part of life do I want to experience that I have never had the opportunity to experience before?

For the first time ever, I had real options. Fortunately, or unfortunately, it took our losing everything to bring us to this point. I had nothing to lose by opening my mind and letting any and all options flood in. I felt totally liberated to consider every opportunity. As I let myself open up to the possibilities, one thought popped up for recognition—a split-second thought from 20 years earlier during my marathon days.

Just run across the United States.

In that split second, it felt right. The timing was perfect. I suddenly had all the time in the world. I was unemployed with no job prospects. We were going to lose our house whether we had jobs or not. I owned my car. Everything else we needed to cross the country was incidental in my mind. The mission statement was all I needed—"just run 20 miles a day for 120 days." Just wake up every morning and do what you love to do, except just keep creeping along across the country. That was it; all I needed to do.

The where, when, how, money, logistics, and support were minor details that could be worked out either beforehand or as we proceeded into the run. Sheryl and I had a lot of obstacles to overcome as we moved across the country, but we always said, "We'll figure it out." And we did. Things just seemed to fall into place as we trekked across the U.S. I took the role of the dreamer and runner. Sheryl, as usual, continued as the practical overseer and sensible counterweight during the adventure.

Sheryl's aunt passed away when we were in western New Mexico. As we drove to Socorro, New Mexico, on a Saturday night, we discussed what we would do about the funeral.

Sheryl wanted to drop everything and fly out of Albuquerque to New York. I immediately thought of the huge cost of last-minute tickets and—the worst part—taking a leave from running. I had just begun to sniff the Pacific. I was into my sixth of eight states and really feeling physically strong and healthy. I had only about 700 miles to go. Now, I would have to put the run on hold which I found very frustrating.

I realized how selfish this was, so I even considered Sheryl's going to New York for the funeral and my continuing without her, camping out along the way. The more I thought about it, the less practical it became; running with a sleeping bag, food, water, and some kind of power for my cell phone to recharge. There were too many things to deal with and no reasonable solutions.

Fortunately, the problem was resolved when Sheryl's cousin politely told her not to come to the funeral. It would be very small and he understood our financial, as well as logistical, situation. This eased the guilt Sheryl was feeling, and we continued. I did feel bad about viewing this from a very selfish standpoint. This event made it crystal clear to me just how important this run was. I was very selfish; I recognized it and admitted it to Sheryl.

It reminded me of an incident in Boston. We had just moved there in 1985, and on a Friday afternoon in June I came home early. We were going to our first Red Sox game at Fenway Park. I was so fired up. *Oh my gosh, my first visit to famous Fenway.* I ran up the stairs to change clothes and saw Sheryl lying on the floor crying. I stopped in my tracks and said, "What's wrong?" Sheryl said Suzie, her little sister, and Richard, her new husband, had just been hijacked on their return flight from Greece. They were on their honeymoon. After the shock wore off, I remember looking at the clock and wondering to myself, "I wonder if this incident can be resolved in an hour and a half. We can still make the game. "

I didn't verbalize that very selfish thought, but it was there. What did I know about terrorist hijackings? Plus it was my first visit to Fenway. I quickly came to my senses and got back to reality.

I did tell Sheryl those thoughts years later. She wasn't surprised. Tunnel vision distorts a proper response to reality.

I think she was also relieved that we were given "permission" by her sister and cousin to miss the funeral.

Realistically, in the end, I would have done whatever we needed to do with respect to Sheryl's family. We would have both gone; I would have just dealt with the brief hold on the run. It wouldn't have been the end of the world for me. It worked out, just as most everything we were confronted with worked out. Even our 11-year-old car held together with a major dose of luck—except in Austin, Texas.

We had reached Austin and I was almost at the end of my day's run. It was a Friday and I heard my cell phone ring. Normally, I ignored calls when I was running, but I was getting ready to take a photo. The caller ID said it was Sheryl. I answered and she told me that the car was smoking and the steering wheel was locked.

I couldn't believe it. I was five miles away from the hotel, Sheryl was at the mercy of an auto repair shop, it was late on a Friday, and we were in a strange city where we didn't know anyone.

My first thought was that we were going to get reamed on the repairs. A woman in an 11-year-old car, stranded. I just pictured the mechanic writing up the estimate with a smile on his face.

As it turned out, he was actually very nice. The cost of the part and repair was high, but it seemed reasonable for what the problem was, and the run back to the hotel was only an additional five miles. I figured we were actually pretty lucky considering that just two days before that we were in the middle of nowhere, between Houston and Austin.

Plus, the car broke down right in front of a European auto repair shop. We didn't need to be towed. All in all, considering it could have been a true nightmare, we were very fortunate.

Our only other mechanical issue was a flat tire when we were going through, of all places, Goodyear, Arizona. We actually drove over 16,000 miles so I could run 2,350 miles—very inefficient by any standard. Maybe, but it was necessary considering the sparse population and scarcity of motels from West Texas to the Pacific coast.

We were driving as many as 300 miles a day so I could run 20. Noah Coughlin, another USA crosser I met, had to fly in eight different drivers along his route during his Transamerica run.

As I progressed through my marathon days, between 1989 and 1996, and then my run across the US, I found myself acquiring new and diverse perspectives on life. My perception of myself and of my relationships with other people, went through many changes.

I feel very fortunate that long ago I realized that if I wanted to get as much out of life as I possibly could, I had to do one thing to begin the process. I had to look in the mirror and be honest with myself. That was the first and most important step. This book is for everyone who wants to view himself and his place in life in a more positive light. My doing so has led to a much more enjoyable and fulfilling life for me.

The following chapters address issues that I contemplated over my miles and miles of running. I consider myself fortunate that I was in a position to devote so much time to thinking, analyzing, and self-reflection, while doing the one thing I love to do—run.

I am not as audacious or delusional as to think that I have the answers to life. I can only say that from where I came from, to where I am today, I am a much more content, satisfied, and mentally healthy person—emotionally and psychologically. This happened because I had the good fortune to take an opportunity to look at myself and the world from a different vantage point during the solitude of running alone.

I couldn't have done this with all the interference we normally have in our daily lives—TV, radio, computers, work, kids, i-this, and i-that. There actually is entertainment in just being alone with one's thoughts. It's an acquired enjoyment; one that comes from a different slant on life and a unique definition of what personal pleasure is.

CHAPTER TWO

An Abbreviated Training Period

After deciding to run across the country, I had to plan my training. I knew I was not in shape because I hadn't run much during the previous six months. Also, over the past two years, with our business not doing well, I hadn't been in a "running" frame of mind.

I didn't put a time frame together because any planning was moot if I couldn't run 20 miles daily. From a physical standpoint, my biggest concerns were my knees and hips. Although I had had arthroscopic surgery on my left knee in 1984—the result of a skiing injury—that was not my main concern. My fear was that at age 60, with over 5,000 miles under my belt, I might be very susceptible to injuries during a 2,350-mile run.

I saw TV commercials for hip and knee replacements. All the actors appeared to be around my age. I was convinced the medical profession knew something that I didn't—that when you turned 60, your knees and hips begin to naturally deteriorate, regardless of your physical conditioning.

I wasn't worried from a mental standpoint. I thought I had the psychological strength to overcome impending obstacles and to enjoy myself during the process. I already had the "training" in that area from preparing for and running seven marathons.

It all came down to my body. Could it endure 2350 miles at 20 miles a day, over a five and a half month time period, under all conditions? That was the big question.

On December 26, 2010, Sheryl and I left on a trip to Estero, Florida, to visit our friends Robin and Paul for a week. They had been wanting us to come down to their winter home in South Florida for years, but because of the store and the time we put in there, we could never pull ourselves away for a visit. We planned to stay until January 1 and then drive up to Orlando to go to the Citrus Bowl to watch Alabama play Michigan State.

I thought this stay in South Florida would be an excellent opportunity to run and check out my body. I always brought my running stuff when we travelled, so I knew Sheryl wouldn't be suspicious. I had no intention of telling her my idea of running across the country—yet.

The weather was a bit chilly when we arrived on Monday, December 27, so I made my first trial run on Wednesday. I wasn't going to get my hopes up; I knew I had a long way to go before I could take that first step toward San Diego. There were a lot of logistics that had to be addressed before it was a reality.

But the first step was to take that first step. And that first step was happening on Wednesday morning. The weather was beautiful. I got up, put on my running clothes, walked out the front door to the end of the driveway, set my watch, and was off.

I don't warm up or stretch; I just start to run. It's probably not the correct way to begin a run, but it's worked for me for over 20 years. After about 50 yards, my hip started to hurt a little. My hip had never hurt before and I remember thinking, well, that was a short-lived dream. I can't even run 50 yards without my hip hurting—Damn!

I decided to push it and see what happened. As I continued, I became sore but decided that, considering I hadn't run much for more than six months, I was doing okay. The discomfort in my hip seemed to gradually disappear.

After a while, I got into my normal rhythm and, although I was sore, I felt pretty good. I attributed the soreness to being out of condition and not to anything serious. I know my body very well and can sense when pains or discomfort needs attention or can be ignored. I was feeling so good that anything that cropped up that Wednesday, I felt could just be ignored.

Normally, in my younger, pre-60 years, I could easily run six miles in an hour regardless of how long it had been since the previous run. Six miles in an hour seemed to be my natural baseline pace. I was always amazed in the spring, after taking the entire winter off, that I could just go outside and run six miles in an hour without a problem. I was always sore but I actually enjoyed that little discomfort. It made me feel that my muscles were still alive and kicking, a way of letting me know that everything was okay.

I completed my run back at the mailbox in front of our friend's house. As I've done for over 20 years, I ended by touching the mailbox and stopping my watch. Seventy minutes. Not bad for my inaugural test run. No major pain. And my hips and knees were non-factors.

I felt great! I passed the first test. I walked inside and Paul asked, "How was the run?"

"Great!"

I got a glass of water and went out to sit by their pool and relax and think about tomorrow's run. I forget what we did that day, but I was already looking forward to running the next day.

Thursday morning I was up and out the door before anyone else was moving about. It was another perfect day. As I opened the door, I thought, if they only knew what this was all about, they'd think I was out of my mind.

I smiled and shut the door behind me. Once again, I walked to the end of the driveway and was off. I ignored the soreness and ran onto the main road to begin an 80-minute run. I would check the miles later when I was in the car by myself and could measure the distance with the odometer.

For now, the priority was time. Running for 80 minutes, regardless of speed, was the immediate goal. Speed was never my priority, but staying in motion for a certain period of time was. The longer I could run without stopping or walking, the more in shape I became. It was pretty simple. Just keep moving: the distance as well as the conditioning will come.

Conditions were perfect: a totally flat surface along a perfectly straight, wide sidewalk. I ran 40 minutes, turned around, and ran back. At this stage, it took 43 minutes to return. I was slower because I wasn't in shape. But, no worries; I felt good and there were no issues with hips or knees. Sore muscles were never a concern at this early stage of training.

Day two of the test was great. I walked into the house, got a glass of ice water, and sat by the pool.

Now I was beginning to get a little fired up. I began to dream of the run, but only for a few moments. I wasn't going to get too excited and overconfident. A lot remained to get through.

Day three was New Year's Eve, and I was happy that on this day, one of the early days of winter, I was able to walk outside in nothing but a short sleeve shirt and shorts, and run.

It was another magnificent day. This was my final run on the trip, and I planned to run for an hour and a half. I was feeling good, still a little sore, but nothing to worry about. I ran 45 minutes out and 50 minutes back. A little slow, but I felt great. I figured I had gone about nine miles. I didn't even care about clocking the distance. Did it really matter? After six months of inactivity, to be able to run for 95 minutes was priceless! I was really beginning to feel that my dream run across the United States was actually going to happen.

As I walked into the house, Paul's future son-in-law asked how my run had been. I said, "Great." Paul chuckled. I'm sure he was thinking I always said every run was great. This one in particular, was.

It was New Year's Eve and, despite losing the business and my mother passing away two months earlier, I felt that 2011 was going to be a very good year—my year of The Run. We had a nice New Year's dinner at Robin and Paul's house and went to bed well before 12:00. At 60, who cares about watching the clock strike midnight? We had an Alabama bowl game to get to tomorrow and I was going to run across the country in 2011.

We got up at dawn to head to Orlando for the game, a four-hour drive. The entire trip, I must have said only about 10 words to Sheryl. Long silences weren't unusual for me, and Sheryl was used to it, knowing I was somewhere else. She was more right than she knew; I was planning my 20-mile test run and thinking about the things I needed to take care of from that point on. It was going to be a very good year.

We went to the game and thoroughly enjoyed watching Alabama manhandle Michigan State. After the game, we made our way back to Atlanta. This afforded me about six hours for thinking and planning the run and considering the last hurdle to surmount—the next test—20 miles.

This 20-mile run was critical. I would find out how my body would react to 5 hours of continuous movement. I would be able to determine if my knees, hips, muscles, and lower back would be able to endure the incessant pounding over a 20-mile course. I felt that if I could withstand 20 miles with no conditioning, then I would be fine as I got stronger throughout the run. That obstacle was addressed the following weekend.

After we got home, I spent the next week in the basement reading. Every day I went into my little side room and tried to read for a few hours. I found myself drifting off and thinking about the run. I really needed to get this next hurdle out of the way so I could begin to make plans for the cross-country run.

The following Saturday, Sheryl and I got up early and drove to the Marietta, Georgia, YMCA where our grandson, Ari, was scheduled to play basketball. Ari was almost four, and I looked forward to watching him play, being the proud grandfather that I am. As we were sitting along the wall watching the kids, I looked up. There, above my head was an indoor track. I was so excited, I turned to Sheryl and said, "Look at that great indoor track! That's where I..."

I stopped. She looked at me with a big question mark on her face, like I had lost it.

"So what," she said.

I realized that it was a big deal only to me. I had found where I was going to run 20 miles. I decided that I was going to take the test run the next day. An indoor track just above my head was truly a sign.

Winter in Atlanta is not brutal, but it is a whole lot colder than Estero, Florida, so discovering an indoor track was a good find. If not for the track, I was going to have to get dressed in layers and run outside. I would have done that, but the idea of running indoors was much more appealing. Training for the 1996 Boston Marathon through the dead of a Boston winter made me shy away from any future cold-weather running.

To cover myself, I told Sheryl that I thought I'd come back tomorrow to check out the track. It looked like a nice one. I even walked upstairs and stood on it. I saw a sign that said the track was 1/18 of a mile. I quickly multiplied 18 by 20 and realized I'd better bring my dreams, fantasies, and imagination with me if I was going to run, walk, or crawl around this oval 360 times.

Sunday morning, I got dressed in my shorts and a short sleeve shirt with a long sleeve T-shirt over it. I'd rather be too hot than cold when running. I sneaked into the bathroom and put Vaseline on my feet, which was a necessity for a long run. I couldn't let Sheryl see me put the Vaseline on because she would have wondered why, for just an hour's run. I figured I'd call her after about two hours to tell her I had decided to play basketball after my run to explain the length of time away.

I headed off to the Y at about 9:30 a.m. I had Sheryl's pedometer so I could make sure I was covering the 20 miles. I knew, as hard as I tried, there was no way I'd remember lap after lap for 360 laps. It was cold out, at least for me, so I was glad I was doing this run inside.

As I approached the Y, I saw there were no cars in the parking lot. My first thoughts were I can't believe it. This place is closed? How can a YMCA close its doors? I was just here yesterday.

When I finished catastrophizing, I saw a man waving and yelling that the Y opened at 1:00. I realized I'd have to go home, change clothes, and run outside. I was going to do 20 miles today, no matter what.

As I began my drive home, I remembered that there was an LA Fitness right next to our old store in Marietta. I was going to pass right by there. I'd just run there. Surely they had an indoor track; the place was huge.

I pulled into the parking lot, and it was almost full. It was the usual after-New Year's rush to fulfill resolutions to lose weight and get in shape. I parked and went inside. At the front desk I asked if they had an indoor track. I was surprised when the attendant said no. Then I saw the basketball court in the distance and asked if I could just run around the court for a while (just five hours). He said I could, but I needed to sign a waiver. I signed and headed to the court.

Finally, the time had arrived. This was it. I'd either move ahead with my plans or drop them. This run would tell me if my body was okay to keep moving for four to five hours at a time.

There were a few young people on the court shooting baskets; I was glad—they'd provide a little entertainment over the next few hours. I calculated that it would take me about five hours. I figured my first 20-mile run since training for the Boston Marathon, 15 years earlier, meant I'd be there for a while.

I probably should have gradually increased my runs to 20 miles. I hadn't run much in six months, and the few times I did over the holidays, it was only approximately six, seven, and nine miles. It was a huge leap to 20.

I knew my body and reasoned if I was going to run 2350 miles, I'd have to just make things work for me. What I was planning was not something traditional, so I figured I was right in step with the abnormality of this whole dream. Was it foolish and dangerous for me to try to run 20 miles with so little conditioning? I probably could have planned differently, but I gave myself credit for knowing when to stop. Plus, I was armed with my daily dose of aspirin, blood pressure and cholesterol medicine, and my megaton vitamin D pill. I was ready to proceed.

I set my pedometer to 0.00, started my watch, and was off. I ran slowly—really slowly—but I went around and around and around. I watched kids and adults come and go on the court. Some were good, most were not, but it was entertaining and I kept going. After about three hours, I stopped long enough to walk outside and get a drink of water. I came right back and kept going. At about four hours, I began to get really tired. I saw that I had run or walked about 16 miles.

I kept going, and at 4 hours and 45 minutes I hit 20.1 miles on the pedometer. I stopped. I was soaking wet and I just stood in the corner of the gym. I had done it. I found out what I needed to know.

With very little conditioning, my body was sore but nothing hurt to the point of causing me concern. My knees and hips were intact and the test run was a success. I walked outside and opened my car door. I was really stiff. It took me a while to get into the car. But I felt good. I was on my way to the next step.

The next step was figuring out all the logistics—route, money, web site, charities, publicity, and—the hardest thing of all—telling my wife. These were all minor details, except for telling Sheryl that we were going to run across the country instead of looking for work; that was a tough one. But I'd figure it out. No worries. The only thing that really mattered was the running, and I had just passed the test.

Then I had to get in shape, decide on a route, and pick a starting date. No need to tell Sheryl yet. I planned to run six more times, 15 miles per run. I chose 15 miles because I didn't want to push myself with the 20 miles. I realized I was kind of lucky that I didn't get injured that Sunday. I didn't want to push my luck. Fifteen miles was long enough to get my body used to the time and distance but not so far that I was pushing the envelope. These 15-mile runs would be sufficient to get me on the road in Jacksonville Beach, and from there I'd get in real shape with each day's run.

Sheryl would think that my renewed interest in running regularly was due to having a clear head and no worries, like I had had when the business was sliding. I decided to run twice a week for the next three weeks. I also decided that it was time to tell the one person in the world who would not think that I was crazy—my son Jeffrey. Jeffrey had decided in 2010 to move to Israel and become a citizen. I figured that anyone who would pick up and move to Judea and Samaria—also known as the West Bank—was a person with whom I could discuss this plan without getting a lot of negativity or uncomfortable silences.

JEFFREY TOLD SHERYL, AT MY REQUEST, ABOUT MY CRAZY PLAN. HE WAS THE FIRST TO KNOW WHAT I WANTED TO DO. TOGETHER IN ISRAEL AFTER THE RUN.

On Sunday, January 23, 2011, I Skyped Jeffrey and chit-chatted for a while. I was just about to tell him my plan when Sheryl came into the room. She talked to Jeffrey for a few minutes and then went into the adjacent bedroom to watch TV, which was too close for comfort. I told Jeffrey that I was going to be texting something for him to think about, something that I didn't want the mum to hear us discuss.

He nodded his head in agreement and I texted the following: "I plan to make a Transamerica run across the United States from Savannah to San Diego. It is 2350 miles. I will run 20 miles a day for 117 days. It will take 5½ months. I'll raise money for two charities. Hopefully, I'll get exposure and get a job by the end of the run."

I pressed "Send" and at that moment it became real. I had told someone. I watched Jeffrey's eyes as he scanned across the screen. I saw him read it again. No expression. He finally looked up, gave a little smirk, and began to type. He typed, "Great idea. You need a Web site, Facebook, Twitter, and include a Jewish charity. Please take Saturday off."

Then we stared at each other. He smiled and said that's awesome. I told him we'd talk later, to think about it, and not to say a word to anyone. He nodded okay and we disconnected.

The wheels were now in motion. I was on a mission, and tunnel vision was forming.

Sheryl came in and told me she was going to have one of our nieces help her with her resume, and that we needed to start looking for jobs. She was talking about working at BuyBuyBaby, or just trying to find some kind of job to have some income. I told her I was on the Internet continuing to look. I was not ready to tell her about our wonderful adventure just around the corner.

I got a text from Jeffrey during the next week, telling me that the mum was very sad about our prospects for the future. He said we needed to tell her soon. I told him we'd Skype on Sunday and break the news to her then. I told him I needed him to be the one to tell Sheryl. I just couldn't do it.

Over the past few weeks, I had desperately searched for the right words to say to Sheryl that would softly and painlessly convey to her that for the next 5½ months we would be hopping from one crappy hotel to another as I ran across the country. I just couldn't bear to see the pain on her face as it sank in. She was already beginning to feel dejected and was losing hope.

It really was a ridiculous idea considering our financial situation. We were already three months behind on our mortgage and getting foreclosure letters. We had very little money and zero prospects for employment. Filing bankruptcy was a strong possibility. Now I'm supposed to tell my wife of 39 years and 7 months that we will be homeless as I run across the country, simply to fulfill a dream I had for a split second, 20 years earlier? At that moment I felt very selfish and self-centered. I simply couldn't bring myself to tell her about this plan. So I took the coward's way out. I told Jeffrey that he had to tell her. He agreed to do it. If anyone could sell her on the idea, it was Jeffrey. He is the master of "spin."

On Sunday morning—afternoon in Israel—I Skyped Jeffrey while Sheryl was in another room. I reminded him that he had to tell Sheryl about my plan. Then I called her in. They began their usual chit-chat. There was a pause, and Sheryl looked at Jeffrey and then at me. I gave Jeffrey a look, indicating that this was the moment of truth.

He said, "Mom, you and Dad are going on a five-and-a-half-month vacation. Dad is going to run across the country. It'll be great. You'll get to see eight states and be on vacation for almost half a year."

Sheryl straightened up and just stared at me. I said, "Sheryl, I'll run 20 miles a day. You'll just drop me off and then pick me up later. It'll be great. We'll get to travel across the country, and at the end we'll see Julie (our daughter) in San Diego.

Sheryl moved to a recliner and sat down as if she had been hit in the head with a bat. There were tears in her eyes. It was worse than I had anticipated. I felt horrible. Finally I said, "Sheryl, this has been a dream of mine for over 20 years. What do we have to lose? We've already lost everything. There are no jobs out there. We're going to lose our house with or without jobs. Let's just take a break. We'll figure it all out when we finish."

My wife of almost 40 years looked at me, and I regretted I had ever thought of this. I saw any bit of hope she had vanish.

There was total silence until she turned to the screen and said to Jeffrey, "Jeffrey, do you think this is a good idea?" He said, "Mom, it's an awesome idea, you'll see." Jeffrey closed the deal when he said, "Mom, if necessary, I'll give you and dad my paychecks for the next six months to help pay for the trip. Something good has to come out of this."

After a long silence, I saw, or thought I saw, her final surrender to simply running out of answers as to how to deal with the new condition of hopelessness we now found ourselves in. She stared at me and said, "When are we going to leave?"

It was a done deal. Sheryl was on board and, just in case we needed it, we had a financial cushion from Jeffrey that made things a whole lot easier. I turned to Jeffrey on the monitor and told him that I wanted to leave in three weeks. He argued that we needed at least a month to get the web site, the charities, and publicity in place. I told Jeffrey that the key to the whole thing was that I run 20 miles a day for 117 days (actually later to be 119 days). Without that, nothing else mattered. I didn't want to tell the world about my ridiculous idea and then after a week, find that I had a malfunctioning body that couldn't run 100 miles. I told him we'd talk in a few days. We said our goodbyes and disconnected.

Sheryl looked at me and her eyes said, "You're out of your mind, but I'll go along with it." I began to discuss all the positives and, as we talked, she began to map out what we needed to do with respect to the house, what to bring, clothes, hotels, food, and whom to tell. I noticed her glances at me, and I knew she was on the verge of wanting to tell me what she really thought: "This is the stupidest thing you could have ever thought of, but I'll go along with it because I have no answers about our future." I wanted to keep her talking to divert her attention away from how absurd this idea really was.

I began looking on MapQuest to get a general idea of where I would be going. I considered beginning in Savannah and ending in San Diego, where Julie was living. I thought Savannah would be good because we had close friends who lived there, and we knew the area. During my next conversation with Jeffrey, he said that Jacksonville would be a better starting point because it was a bigger area and I possibly could get more press coverage, which I ended up not getting.

I agreed that made sense, so Jacksonville it was. Well, really Jacksonville Beach on the Atlantic, about 18 miles east of Jacksonville. So, the starting point and ending points were set. Plus, since I was starting in February, the farther south the better, as I preferred running in warm rather than cold conditions.

I went on MapQuest, put in the two points, and up popped my mileage. I initially put in Jacksonville instead of Jacksonville Beach, so the mileage to San Diego was 2341 miles. That was the mileage I used when I discussed the length of my run initially, although in reality it was over 2350 miles. For round numbers sake, I decided to use the 2350 figure. My objective was to run from the Atlantic Ocean to the Pacific Ocean, so to me the exact mileage was secondary. Another mileage variable was that the route on MapQuest was based on I-10. I actually ran on U.S. and state roads parallel to I-10, thus affecting the true mileage again.

I had a hard time using MapQuest, so I decided to just go out and get a printed map of Florida and, subsequently, maps of the rest of the seven states I would run through. I was able to work much better with the old-fashioned printed maps.

That following Tuesday, I went to the YMCA in Marietta and walked up to the track and began my first 15-mile run. It was a run/walk. I finished the 15 miles in about 3½ hours. I was already beginning to feel myself getting stronger.

Despite the huge amount of Vaseline on my feet, I was developing blisters—but no injuries or muscle problems, so, all in all, a very good run. As I ran, I thought of the huge number of miles I'd be running as I crossed the U.S. I decided that the only way to accomplish this run was to take each day's run one day at a time. I had to consider each day as a training run for a marathon. I just had to enjoy the run and not think about the miles or days ahead of me.

The Thursday before we were to leave for Jacksonville, I made my final 15-mile run. I really felt good and strong. As I ran, I started to think of day one of the run, when I would actually touch the Atlantic and head off across the sand to the pavement and begin my run on Route 90, through Florida and into Alabama. I was so excited.

I ran nonstop for three hours. Fifteen miles in three hours, 5 miles per hour, 12-minute miles. I felt great! Not bad for just a few training runs after a six-month absence from running. As I walked to my car, I began to think about my pace. At that rate, I would run 20 miles in four hours. Doing that for 117 days began to concern me. I decided that I needed to pace myself for the long haul. I didn't want to tear up my body. I figured that was a good pace for a run here and a run there, but not for what I was going to do. I also wanted time to take pictures and videos. I was not making this a timed run to the Pacific. It was going to be fun. I needed to slow down, even as I became more conditioned.

I decided I needed to set a slower pace. I would run 13- to 13.5-minute miles and leave some time to walk while drinking and eating if necessary, and to take pictures. I also anticipated hills, mountains, altitude, and intense heat as I progressed west. So, if necessary, I would walk some to minimize the wear and tear and risk of injury. This was not going to be a job. This was going to be fun and entertaining for me. The goal was to run across the country, period. Not run 1,000 miles and collapse.

The last three practice runs, I called Sheryl from the gym to let her know I was okay and I'd be home soon. I could tell in her voice that with each successful training run, she was getting more into this whole adventure. She was asking me about the run, making sure I was not hurt or feeling any strain on my body. I could tell that if I had a problem, she was going to be upset and disappointed. This made me even more determined. Since Sheryl was so supportive and had such a great attitude, I was not going to let anything happen to disappoint her. She really came through for me on this one. I was going to come through for her.

At that moment I knew there were no options but to run into the Pacific Ocean and complete this run. I decided no matter what I went through each day, I would tell Sheryl I had a great run and felt good. I was not going to cause her any concern that we may have to turn around and end the run early. She was so into this now; I was really amazed.

Sheryl had resolved all the details. She made arrangements to have someone stay in our house and to pack it up to move out by June when the bank would be foreclosing. She registered with the hotel chains to get free hotels after a certain number of stays. She made a list of all the numbers to call so we could pay our bills by phone or online. Sheryl packed all our clothes except my running stuff. Food, medicine, drinks—all were taken care of. She bought maps and a notebook so we could document each day where I ended my run.

As it turned out, we over packed and when we got somewhere in Texas we went to a UPS store and sent more than half our clothes home.

CHAPTER **3** THREE

Getting the Word Out

Once I had finished my 20-mile run and my six 15-mile runs, I set the starting date at February 14, Valentine's Day. Could there be a better Valentine's gift to my wife than a 5½-month run across the country? I was then ready to tell a few people who needed to know what we were doing. I needed to tell my siblings and my kids and attempt to tell my father whose health was failing quickly. We decided not to tell anyone else, for good reason.

We drove to Birmingham to tell my older brother and twin sister about our plans. I also wanted to sit down with my father and try to tell him, realizing that it would be difficult because his mental capacity was diminishing by the week. He was in a nursing home.

But, on second thought, while sitting with my father, I decided to make a second trip back to Birmingham specifically to say goodbye to him just before we left for Jacksonville. I felt it was going to be my last goodbye, and I wasn't ready for it yet.

In Birmingham, as I was sitting in my brother's den, he asked me if we had thought about any plans for the future. I told him that we did know what we were doing. I said that I was making a Transamerica run from Jacksonville to San Diego, 2350 miles, 20 miles a day. I included that I'd be raising awareness about the very bad employment situation in the country, especially for baby boomers. We would also be raising money for two charities: United Way and Nefesh B'Nefesh.

He looked at me in silence; a very long silence. I knew my brother was not only trying to relate to what I had just said, but also was looking for an appropriate response. Initially he said, "I had thought of a few things you might be telling me, but this wasn't one of them." From that point on I realized that whatever he said was going to be diplomatic. I explained that it was something I had wanted to do and this was a good time.

He really didn't know what to say. It was at that moment that I realized just how unusual and unorthodox this whole idea was. These past few months, thinking of this run, I had never looked at the "oddness" of it. To me, it was just an incredible challenge. I hadn't thought of it from an "outsider's" perspective.

His response, or rather lack of response, was, I guess, understandable. The questions my brother did ask were all legitimate and certainly reasonable and logical.

But they were questions about details that I wasn't really prepared to answer; they were minor issues, not yet addressed, but easily planned for. I only knew one thing: I was going to run across our United States. All the other stuff—details—would be worked out when the time was right. I had simply come to let my brother and sister know where I'd be for the next five and a half months.

The next morning at breakfast, I told my twin sister and sister-in-law. Again, I was met with silence and shock. It became obvious that, except for my father and other brother and my two other kids, we were not going to discuss our plans with anyone else. I realized that everyone was at a loss as to how to respond to what we were going to do. I wasn't going to go through this again with other family members and friends. I was very uncomfortable, for them and for me. I knew I could and would make the complete run, but I also knew that everyone else simply couldn't relate to what I was about to do.

Sheryl and I decided that after I had run the first 100 miles, and things looked promising, we would send an email to other family members and our friends. Since we'd closed the store, friends and family were all genuinely concerned about our future plans, so we did feel a sense of obligation to make everyone aware of our next step. Sending our news via email might seem cowardly, but at least this way people would have a chance to digest the information and have time to think of a response.

We decided this was best for everyone involved. I didn't realize the shock quotient of saying "I'm going to run across the country." The truth is, I hadn't thought about what their response would be or the impact it would have on people we told. This is the e-mail we sent to friends and family:

To friends and family,

In October of last year, Sheryl and I had to close our business after 12 years due to our country's economic decline. We've weathered many recessions in our 37 years in business, but this current recession/depression cost us everything. To keep our business afloat the last two years we put everything we had into it. Since October we have tried to find employment, but realized that in this economic climate it is difficult for so many, but particularly for those at our age.

Rather than spin our wheels, we decided to turn the pain and discomfort of unemployment into a constructive purpose that will benefit people in similar circumstance. At the same time, I am fulfilling a twenty-year dream of mine of running across the United States.

This past Monday, February 14th, I began my Transamerica run from Jacksonville, Florida, to San Diego, California, 2341 miles from the Atlantic to the Pacific Ocean. I plan to run 20 miles a day which will take about 120 running days. I will not be running on Saturdays out of respect for our Sabbath.

The purpose of this run is twofold: First, I am hoping to raise awareness of the severe unemployment problem in this country, in particular, for those of our age, the baby-boomers. Second, at the same time we will be raising money for two charities whose primary mission is to help those looking for a new start. The United Way 211 program that helps those who have lost their jobs and need immediate assistance, and Nefesh B'Nefesh, a Jewish organization that offers assistance to Jews all over the world who want to settle in Israel.

Both charities and Mr. Scott Sakoff, a media marketing executive, will be handling exposure for my run. This will be the exposure needed to assist these charities.

On a personal note, I am asking for your help in supporting the run itself by donating at the bottom of the Support the Cause page to "Richard's Run Fund." Your donation will help defray the cost of hotels, gas, food, laundry, etc.

Please visit the Web site www.20AT60.com to learn more about the run and to help any way you can. All donations are greatly appreciated. Please pass this on to your friends and family via e-mail, Facebook, Twitter, and verbally.

Thank you,

Richard and Sheryl Cohen

We went to Birmingham for the second and final time before we left for Jacksonville. I needed to say good-bye to my father, possibly for the last time. He was approaching 93 and his health, more mental than physical, had deteriorated rapidly since my mother had passed away three months earlier. He had fallen a number of times and was suffering from brain bleeds. He was beginning to exhibit the effects.

During our last trip to Birmingham, before beginning my run, Sheryl and I went directly to the nursing home to visit my father. I asked if I could be alone with him. Sheryl left the room and, as I stood at my father's bedside, I knew this could very well be the last time I would see him alive. I had no idea where I'd be on my run if and when the call came that he had passed away or was close to death.

His eyes were closed, and I don't know if he heard what I said. He was unable to speak. I told him that I loved him and that he had been a really good father to me. I said the Shema, the prayer that should be the final prayer a Jewish person says or hears. I kissed him and stood there rubbing his hand. I was finding it hard to believe that after sixty years, this moment had come and it was probably the last time I would see my father alive.

Standing there, I recalled some happy childhood memories: Going to Maxwell Air Force Base every weekend in the summer to swim, eat dinner and go to a movie; pizza at Tony's; the many trips to New York to visit family in the summer; his laughing at me when I saw a tow truck with 'Wrecker' painted on the side and asked if that truck wrecks your car for you; visitor's day at Camp Rotary.

I smiled as I remembered the times before my bar mitzvah, sitting next to my father in synagogue. I'd tap his watch as a signal that it was time for him to give me his watch so I could have a contest with myself to see how long I could hold my breath. He would occasionally glance at me to make sure I had not passed out.

I laughed to myself as I remembered a family trip to Callaway Gardens where, during a family breakfast in the hotel restaurant, I ordered six eggs—just to piss him off.

As I stood there, rubbing his hand, I looked at him and wondered if, months ago when he was more aware, he had looked back on his life and had any regrets. I wondered if there was anything he really wanted to see or do that he didn't. I hoped not.

The good times flashed by as I spent the last minutes with my dad. He was a good man, a really good man: honorable, nice, decent, humble, intelligent. He taught me values and goodness. I would miss him a lot. I cried.

I told him I was running across the country. I figured it was falling on deaf ears but it made me feel better that I was sharing this with him. As I walked away, I turned and looked at him one last time. I opened the door and walked out. I was sad but I had no regrets. I was always honest with him. He knew exactly how I felt. He appreciated that. I had been a good son.

At various times during my run, I thought about what he would have said. I smiled as I pictured him staring at me with his mouth open, saying "What?"

That I could stake my life on. He was hard of hearing and, coupled with his inability to even vaguely comprehend what I was going to do, the plan would have elicited total befuddlement.

As it turned out, I was on the outskirts of west Tallahassee when I called my brother to check on my father's condition. He said that hospice was giving him just a few days longer. We left immediately and got to Birmingham the day before he passed away on Friday evening, February 25.

On that same final visit, we had gone to say good-bye to my brother and sister. When my twin sister and I were saying our good-byes, she hugged me and started to cry. She said if it got too hard for me she wanted me to come home. I said that something very bad would have to happen for me not to finish this run. I had not expected her to cry, so I felt horrible. I wanted to reassure her that I was going to be fine. I wanted to make sure she was okay. Seeing my twin sister cry on my behalf sucked!

CHAPTER **4** FOUR

Telling Our Son

My firstborn son, Jason, acts older and is more mature than I am. He is a typical firstborn.

There was a reason I didn't mention my plans to him earlier. Jason, from the day we closed the store, told me I needed to get my resume out, start networking, spend eight hours a day looking for a job. Not surprising, because that's what he did when he graduated with his MBA a few months earlier.

He created a resume for me and I was very impressed with the array of talents he attributed to me. I appreciated his advice and concern, but following his example just wasn't going to happen. I needed a break before I got back into the real world.

However, we needed to tell him before we left, so we asked Jason and Danielle, our daughter-in-law, to come over. We wanted to say goodbye and see our grandkids one last time before we took off. When they walked in, I motioned to Sheryl to take the kids, and I asked Jason and Danielle to come into the other room.

I told them that I was making a Transamerica run from Jacksonville Beach, to San Diego, 2350 miles, 20 miles a day for about 120 running days. It would take 5½ months.

They both looked at me, stunned and speechless. Danielle was the first to speak. She said, as a courtesy, "Wow! That's unbelievable!" Like Forest Gump? She then asked what we were going to do when we got to San Diego.

I replied, "I guess we'll fly back."

"What will you do with your car?" After realizing that we would have our car and that getting back to the east coast was the furthest thing on my mind, I said, "Oh. I guess we'll drive back."

I was so focused on getting to San Diego, that I had not even addressed the subject of the return trip.

My son, Jason, remained silent during the entire conversation. But I did notice a slight wagging of his head and saw a smirk on his face. I knew what he was thinking. His expression said, "Dad, that's the dumbest thing I've ever heard. You need to be out looking for a job."

His silence stretched on and I decided to end the discomfort by saying we'd be back for my dad's funeral, and we'd certainly not miss Rachel's eighth birthday in March and the school play she was in the day following her birthday. We'd also plan to fly back in May from wherever we were, to attend our niece's wedding in Birmingham.

That was it for them. My unconventional trek across the country was received as I anticipated, with two head shakes and a smirk. It was certainly different from Jeffrey's reaction, but expected.

Our daughter, Julie, only asked when would we arrive in San Diego and could she pick the restaurant to go to for the celebration. She offered to pay for our first visit to In-N-Out Burger if we would pay for the celebration at Ruth's Chris. I told her it would be my pleasure.

I know my kids; they reacted just as anticipated. Jeffrey was excited about the prospects of a great adventure for us. Jason was concerned about our well-being and the need to provide an income for ourselves. Julie was looking forward to the visit. Between the three of them, we got to embrace the full range of perspectives on our quirky adventure.

JASON, DANIELLE, RACHEL AND ARI. DAILY CALLS TO CHECK ON US.

Change

There are important things in your life and there are urgent things in your life. Urgent things, such as earning money, taking care of the kids, upkeep on the house, insurance, etc., are what we find ourselves attending to daily. The important things, such as mental health, psychological strength, developing healthy coping skills, feeling content and fulfilled seem to be set aside for "later." Later usually slips into years and decades, and then never.

The upside to hitting rock bottom is that you have plenty of time to revisit the important things in your life. You really do have nothing to lose by attending to the real issues that make life complete. In the case of losing everything, the new condition offers an opportunity to change perspective. You have to recognize the opportunity and look at the benefits, instead of trying to adjust your old values to a new condition.

A change in perspective is different from a change of scenery. People today who find themselves unhappy or stuck or simply lost sometimes think a move to a new city, or a change in relationships, or a change in careers will bring about either a change to happiness or getting unstuck or even finding oneself.

The scenery may change but the eyes don't. Change comes from getting a new set of lenses and filters and a new way of interpreting life. A change in relationships only brings a new face to dump the old baggage onto. A change of locale only gives a new address to the same old perspective.

When Sheryl and I closed the business and decided to make this run across the country, we wiped the slate clean of old values and perspectives. We saw this as an adventure and a chance to see the country during our very slow trek across the U.S. We could have easily ignored the opportunity and just trudged along looking for any employment and trying desperately to hang on to our old lifestyle.

However, we were fortunate enough to see the possibilities and to decide that we would enjoy the journey. We wouldn't worry about what might lie ahead after the run. Our shift in attitude and perspective affected how we approached life from that point on. Our values changed from things and routines to activities and an ability to embrace the unknown.

This run truly was an adventure. We helped each other gain new perspective and found ourselves looking ahead, not behind. We loved and cherished our past; we had great memories. But this was the start of a new life for us, beginning with a 2,350 mile run across the country.

I ran each day. Sometimes we didn't know where we would spend the night. Dots on the map occasionally turned out to be ghost towns. We got used to it and saw it as a challenge and adventure. Our conditions changed and, out of necessity, we adapted with the change. We didn't fight it or try to get back to the "old days." We adjusted to new conditions and saw irony and humor in it all.

We were two well-educated adults who went from owning a very comfortable 5000-square-foot home and a successful business, to living out of a car, going from one hotel room to another, while I ran 20 miles a day. For the two of us, it was so absurd it was actually amusing.

Change can come about as a conscious effort to alter a behavior, or it can come as a way of adapting to a changing environment. In any event, changing one's behavior isn't easy. To bring about real change, you must first alter your point of view and your priorities.

If you realize you are overweight, you must change your attitude: change your view of the value of food and then change your eating habits. Change involves the continual, conscious effort to eliminate an undesired behavior and replace it with a more desirable, appropriate and, eventually, comfortable one. Change needs motivation, discipline, self-control, and the real desire and need to avoid the pain and discomfort associated with the undesirable behavior. You also have to continually weigh the cost of the effort to change—is it really worth the effort to change? Most people, unfortunately, don't think so and fall back to their familiar behavior.

If you have done well on your diet and lost 10 pounds but you have a big wedding weekend coming up, the question becomes "Do I stay on my diet and forego the good eats, or can I really just enjoy myself for this weekend? How much will the added effort and discipline cost me? Will it cost me even more in the long run?" It's your choice.

Reality is reality. The only thing that changes reality is one's perception of it. If faced with a reality that is unchangeable, the only thing to do in order to accept a reality is to adapt and change how it is perceived. If a man loses his leg in war, the reality is that he has but one leg. He can either get depressed and feel like a partial man with no future or he can change his view and interpretation of the situation, decide to get a prosthetic leg, learn how to function with it, and live a relatively normal life. Is it 100 percent the same? No, but a change in how the missing leg is perceived is a viable healthy alternative to depression, isolation, and self-pity.

As it turned out, I had to deal with reality and perspective fairly early in the run. I was running over the bridge entering Pascagoula, Mississippi, heading west, and I was feeling fine on the ascent to the crown of the bridge. As I descended, I automatically picked up speed, very happy and relieved to have a brief downhill run. Then I became aware of a pain in the front of my leg, just above my foot. I slowed down but it got worse. By the time I finished my run I could barely walk. I then noticed a huge knot at the point where my foot attaches to my lower leg. The pain was excruciating.

I was in only my third state. This was my first real challenge of the run. I had no insurance or I would have gone to an orthopedist or podiatrist. As I sat in the hotel room looking at my leg, I got frustrated and angry. I had no idea what this injury was or how to treat it. Should I put ice on it—or heat? I didn't know. I tried ice but it didn't help. For the rest of the day, I limped around trying to figure out what to do. Sheryl and I went to a drug store and got two types of Ace bandages. I'd try them and ibuprofen.

The next morning the pain was just as bad. Neither of the Ace bandages helped. Sheryl insisted that I not run that day so I could rest my leg. It killed me not to run, but I took the day off.

The next day, I woke up with no relief but I got dressed and told Sheryl I'd just figure it out as I ran. She begrudgingly dropped me off where I had concluded my previous run, and off I limped. I knew if I altered my steps and stride, it could lead to even bigger problems. So I just kept on and tried to ignore the pain.

I slowed my pace, but it didn't offer any relief. I also noticed that my ankles were swelling. I managed to finish my 20 miles for that day, but I was totally spent; mentally and physically. It took just about everything I had to bear the pain and stay focused on maintaining my stride. I tried ice again that night but it didn't help.

I knew I had to work through this. I had already weighed the cost of quitting. It was way too high a price for me to even consider as an option. I envisioned the long drive home having not reached the Pacific. It would have been a major letdown and disappointment for us both. In my mind, the pain of stopping outweighed the physical pain of my leg.

This was my challenge: I had placed the cost of quitting so high that I had to either find a solution or just run in pain. For the next seven running days, I ran in pain. I almost became used to it. The pain didn't decrease; I just managed to adapt and accept it as an annoyance.

When we got to Slidell, Louisiana, Sheryl suggested that I elevate my legs, to help the swelling. I thought back to my days in high school running track. I remembered seeing runners lying next to walls with their legs elevated against the wall. I never did that, but maybe there was something to it.

RESTING MY LEGS IN SLIDELL, LOUISIANA.

I used a lounge chair by the pool and lay reversed with my head at the foot and my legs resting on the back of the chair. I'll be damned; it worked! The swelling went down and even the large walnut-sized knot above my foot felt a little better.

After that, we realized that the swelling may have been caused by the high-cut black Nike socks I was wearing. They could have been constricting the flow of blood from my lower legs. I remembered noticing when I took my socks off those past few days, that there was an indentation in my leg where the elastic band of the sock was digging into it. This was later confirmed by a salesperson at Luke's Locker, a running store in Houston. She said the blood was puddling in my feet and not going back up my legs.

We bought very low-cut socks from the girl's department at Walmart. They had pink toes and were perfect. I still had pain in my leg from the knot, but it was beginning to subside. By the time we got to Houston, Texas, it was much better and I was hoping for some pain-free runs.

While in Houston we had the good fortune to spend the first night of Passover with a Cantor whose wife was an acupuncturist. She offered to apply her skills to my leg, which I declined at first, but at Sheryl's urging, I agreed and called her the next day. I had never considered acupuncture, but she was nice enough to open her office for me. She did her sticking and poking, and I have to say, my leg felt better. From that point (no pun intended) on, I was pain free. The knot shrank, and I ran without pain all the way to San Diego. I still have a small knot on my leg, but no pain; just a small reminder of my run.

The priority of running to the Pacific was so strong, that I was able to view the pain and discomfort of my leg injury from a different perspective. I gave it little value and very little attention while running, after the first few days. The change came in how I viewed and interpreted the injury. I adapted to the change in conditions and accepted the new situation in which I found myself.

You have to put a value on the change you want to realize. Is the value of looking and feeling better greater than the brief pleasure of that chocolate éclair? Finishing the run was more important to me than the relief of the pain in my leg. These are the kinds of choices that have to be made during the process of change. Are you disciplined enough to get through the temptations of temporary relief or brief pleasure?

Change can sometimes be brought about by a traumatic event in one's life. In 1985, my sister-in-law and her husband were on a hijacked flight returning from their honeymoon in Greece. Her experiences of those days living in terror changed the course of her and her husband's life. The biggest change, in her case, was to her priorities—what she considered important and unimportant. From that point on her religious beliefs and convictions became her new guide through life. One can never know if the new direction is better or not, only that it will lead down a different path.

Whatever the impetus, change will come if it becomes a priority greater than the need to maintain the status quo.

Our store had been next door to an LA Fitness. Every January the parking lot was packed with cars because people had made their New Year's resolutions to lose weight and get in shape. Noble indeed. In February, the parking lot was less full. By April, there were few cars in the lot.

It was totally predictable. Everyone makes resolutions, but it is only a small handful who actually follow through on the change they resolved to make. Only a few realize it is more important to make a change in their lives than anything else that they could be doing with their time. These are the people who are truly dedicated to bringing about change.

In order to be successful with changes, one needs confidence and faith in oneself to persevere through the process. Success breeds success. If you start off with small changes, building your confidence and psychological strength, you will build the ability for bigger challenges and more dramatic changes.

My love of running distances began with my first 15-minute run on a treadmill, in my basement, in Boston during the winter of '88-'89. By March, I was running up to 45 minutes nonstop. As soon as the weather warmed up, I was outside running much farther.

I saw the progress I was making and it gave me the strength and desire to go farther. From that small 15 minute success, I ran my first marathon.

I had fun and felt great. The successes led me to want more. I was never satisfied, so I ran six more marathons. And then I had the crazy idea that it would be awesome to run across the country. Recognizing one's strengths is as important as finding the flaws that need changing. Don't be afraid to give yourself credit where credit is due. A person needs psychological strength and confidence in order to know he or she can succeed in making changes, one of the most important aspects of healthy coping skills.

Change is really about overcoming the desire to stay the same, despite the discomfort it causes. Whether you want to lose weight, change careers, get out of a relationship, or fulfill a dream, it takes strength to move from the comfort of familiarity and habit; it is a battle to break old perspectives.

How many times do we eat even if we aren't really that hungry? Eating becomes a habit and is situational. Whenever I went to the movies, I automatically got popcorn and a drink. I wasn't hungry, but the movie experience always included food. When I decided to lose weight, I changed how I perceived the value of eating. It became a lower priority to me because an even bigger priority was the satisfaction of looking and feeling better.

I had to fight the habit of continually seeing food and eating it as an enjoyable activity. I learned to view it as something detrimental to my plan to look and feel better, which I gave a much higher value to. As days passed, my old habit grew weaker and my new attitude about what food and eating meant to me slowly became my new normal—and I lost the weight I wanted. Determination, discipline, and self-control were factors that played equal parts in the process.

I mention the habit of eating because eating too much, smoking, drinking, and using drugs are compulsions that seem to cause the most distress in Americans' lives. Probably more time, energy, and money are spent trying to get these issues under control than any other compulsive behaviors in our society.

Positive change yields personal growth that leads to being more content with yourself. When you like yourself, then others like you, too, and relationships become healthier. It is an upward spiral that only gets better.

CHAPTER **6** SIX

The Run Begins

On February 13, 2011, Sheryl and I packed up the car and headed to Jacksonville. I was excited and felt free and unencumbered for the first time in years. What we had in the car was all we were going to have at our disposal for the next five and a half months.

I felt like I was Martin Luther King giving his "Free at Last" speech in Washington. No store to worry about, no people to deal with. Financial problems, yes, but we were good for a while, especially with Jeffrey's promised help. My kids were all safe and happy; all had jobs and were in good places. It was just me and Sheryl heading out to run across the country.

At age 60, we were retiring for five and a half months. We had enough money for a month or so and we had Jeffrey's paychecks as a backup if we needed them. I wasn't worried. I really believed that everything was going to work out, that something good had to come out of a 60-year-old man's run across the United States. What we were doing was a good thing, at least for us. When you have nothing to lose, you might as well enjoy the light load.

As I drove, I was daydreaming about the run: 20 miles a day, each day, day after day. I can do that. It beats the stress of work, that's for sure. It would be just me and the open road—2350 miles of it. I knew the only thing that mattered was my physical health. Everything else would take care of itself: money, publicity, hotels, food, etc. I had to stay fit, healthy and injury free for 119 days of running. If I could do that, I'd be hugging Julie in the Pacific.

When Sheryl and I arrived in Jacksonville that afternoon, we checked into the first of 56 different hotels along the way, a total of 144 nights in hotels and motels over the entire run. It was a nicer-than-average Best Western. After we got settled, I wanted to drive to Jacksonville Beach to see where I was going to start my run the next morning, Valentine's Day. We had planned to wake up early in order to be at the beach before the sun

FEBRUARY 14, 2011, VALENTINE'S DAY – EARLY MORNING, JACKSONVILLE BEACH, AS THE SUN RISES, I BEGIN MY TRANSAMERICA RUN ACROSS THE UNITED STATES.

came up so we could video my start with the sun rising behind me. I thought that would be a fitting way to begin our journey. A new day; a new beginning. Perfect.

The next morning, we woke up at 5:45. According to The Weather Channel, sunrise was at 7:06 a.m. I wanted to be there early to see the sunrise and have Sheryl video the sun coming up. I wanted Sheryl to record my touching the Atlantic Ocean and heading away from the beach towards the road: Route 90 West. It was cold, but worth the wait as the sun began to peek over the horizon. The video on my web site shows me waiting for the sun to rise, wishing everyone a happy Valentine's Day, putting my foot in the water, and beginning my first day of running.

FEBRUARY 13 – SHERYL IS FIRED UP AND READY TO HEAD DOWN TO JACKSONVILLE FOR THE BEGINNING OF THE RUN ON VALENTINE'S DAY.

I remember clearly, thinking as I ran through the sand, that this was the start of the next five and a half months. I took a deep breath and said to myself, "Okay, let's get this done." Then I thought about running into the Pacific, having run 2350 miles. It was a very brief moment of feeling anxious and wanting to get to that ending point. I used the image of hugging Julie as we stood in the Pacific Ocean to propel me daily. Nothing was going to keep me from meeting this challenge which I had put to myself.

I stepped off the sand onto the side street leading from the beach, ran a short distance, and got onto Route 90 heading west towards Jacksonville. The first day was beautiful. It was a little chilly and surface streets took me into downtown Jacksonville; over the bridges, into the western part of the city, and beyond.

My run was now a reality.

CHAPTER SEVEN

My Evolving Daily Routine

After my first few days of running I found my morning preparation evolving into a comfortable routine. Despite enjoying the freedom of not having a normal daily routine as I had when working, I did need to follow a mental checklist before I set out to run each day.

Each morning I woke up on my own; no alarm clock to force me to get up at a certain time. I did this because I wanted my sleep to be open-ended and not specific. I knew I needed a good night's sleep every night and I also knew that when I had to get up at a certain time, I had a miserable night's sleep for fear of not hearing the alarm and oversleeping. So, I got up when I was ready. Even later in the run when I was in intense heat, in west Texas and beyond, I decided not to get up extra early to "beat the heat" because to me running at 7:30 a.m. when the temperature was already 90 degrees was really no advantage over running at 5:30 a.m. in 85 degrees. With temps a few hours later at 112, did it really matter? Hot as hell is hot as hell.

So every morning I got up and went to the bathroom, and then put my shorts on, a long-sleeved shirt, and a short-sleeved shirt. Next I put Vaseline all over the bottom of my feet and between my toes—not just a little, but gobs. Then I turned my socks inside out and put them on. The outside of these socks were softer than the inside. I made sure my shoes were nearby so I didn't have to walk across the room leaving a trail of Vaseline squeezing through my socks. I wiped my hands on a towel and put my shoes on, double tying the laces. I hated having to stop to bend over to tie my laces when I ran.

I made sure the night before that my cell phone was plugged in to recharge. I put my small carrying belt on with $7, mace, a small pointed steel leaf (as a pathetic excuse for a weapon) and my phone in the pouch. I grabbed my sunglasses (only from Tahoka, Texas, on, after the dust storm) and hat, and put my watch on, and then Sheryl was up and we headed out.

Each day before I finished my run, we noted in our notebook the exact spot I ended. Sometimes we had to use nearby landmarks like a mailbox or a tree or a fence or house to note the spot. We also used the car's odometer to mark off distance from the hotel or an intersection or mile marker.

As we approached the spot to begin my run, I'd pull off the road and get out of the car. I'd come around to Sheryl's side and get a can of sunscreen and spray my face and neck. During a stretch of running in western New Mexico and eastern Arizona, I also had to spray fly repellant all over myself. The flies in that area were horrible. Also, in that area I had to make sure I brought my surgical mask to wear because of the smoke from the fires in southeast Arizona, blowing my way.

I checked myself and Sheryl checked me to make sure I had all my stuff. When we hit western Texas, I switched my belt with a pouch, for a water belt that has a pouch and two ten-ounce water bottles. I filled them with cold water at the hotel, but within an hour the water had reached outside temperature and was not very refreshing. It was only good for keeping me hydrated.

At the Tonopah, Arizona, I-10 exit, I started to use a Camelbak that solved my hydration issues because it was insulated and held 64 ounces of fluid—a real lifesaver.

During my daily run, I would call Sheryl after about 2-2/12 hours to let her know I was okay. I ran at a steady, slow pace to avoid injury and would walk when I was drinking or eating either Fig Newtons from a convenience store stop, or Welch's Berries and Cherries (like gummy bears) that I carried with me.

The wind was brutal in west Texas and New Mexico, virtually always in my face. The hills and higher elevations, up to almost 7700 feet, were very hard to climb, even when I walked. I was also short of breath at the higher elevations.

Each day as I ran, I simply enjoyed the scenery and felt relaxed and content. To occupy myself mentally, I thought up movie scripts. Sometimes I would stop and just look at the scenery and imagine what it was like hundreds of years ago. I was a kid on an amazing adventure to explore the sights and sounds and smells of our country's isolated areas. While running east of Lubbock, Texas, I passed through small towns and saw a lot of people and all that accompanies civilization—stores, houses, animals, honking cars. As I progressed further west, I saw less civilization and more natural, untouched beauty. I found myself stopping more and enjoying it more—just peace and solitude and the time and frame of mind to appreciate it all.

As I ran, I rehashed movie scripts I had begun to mentally write over 20 years ago. I would tweak each story or idea and got further and further into the stories. I would simply run and think and enjoy the surroundings and feel content. I switched back and forth from taking in my surroundings to playing my movies in my head. The time just passed by as I was having the time of my life. The physical activity of actually running became so incidental and so effortless that it was just the secondary activity that I was engaged in.

My Mirror Image

As I was running outside Tallahassee, about 175 miles from Jacksonville Beach, I saw a man in the distance. I could tell he was walking with plastic garbage bags and a bed roll slung over his shoulder. As I approached him, I slowed to a stop and talked to him. This man had walked from California, stopping in towns along the way looking for work. He had crossed the country and was heading back east. He had been travelling on foot for over two years.

He told me that he had travelled the perimeter of the state of Florida looking for work. He was unkempt, unshaven, and wearing wrinkled clothes, but other than that he appeared to have tried to keep as clean as possible. His face was worn, and I'm sure he had not laughed or even smiled in quite a while. He was very thin and the baggage he was carrying was obviously heavy. It held his entire life. In the 1920s he would have been called a hobo.

He told me about how hard it was to find work. I told him I had just lost my business and was running across the United States to raise awareness of the country's huge unemployment problem. He asked me to put a word in for the homeless. He said, "There ain't no jobs out there, anywhere."

As he started to walk away, I shook his hand and asked his name. He said his name was "Richard." I wished him well and resumed my run.

As I headed off, I began to cry. For the first time on our trip, I saw the reality of our situation. No job, no home, very little money, and a huge question mark as to our future. I had let my family down and everyone, especially Sheryl, had to suffer the consequences.

For that brief moment, I felt sorry for myself and began to blame myself for losing the business and putting Sheryl and myself in this situation—hopping from one cheap hotel to the next, in the hopes that someone would notice what I was doing and offer us a job. This run was my version of standing in Times Square holding up a sign that read "Looking for work, please hire me."

For those few moments, I questioned what the hell I was thinking to put myself and Sheryl through this. I stopped and cried because I saw myself in this man's face. I, too, was without work and in reality, homeless. I looked in the mirror and this other Richard, who came out of nowhere, was the reflection looking back at me. The fact that his name was Richard made it even more troubling and so overwhelming that I broke down. Two homeless, jobless Richards passing each other on their trips across the country simply looking for work. It really was too much for me for a few minutes.

I called Sheryl and told her that if she passed this man to stop and give him some food and money. She did pass him and she did stop. I, at least, felt good that we did what we could for this man. I'll never forget him.

A Question of Balance

When I started running years ago, I realized that what I enjoyed was the sense of freedom and solitude of running. I then expanded that thought to realize that it filled me with contentment and I felt fulfilled as an individual, not as a husband, father, or businessman. I realized that up until that point I was directing all my resources towards my family and my business. I began to see an imbalance in my life due to my focus on business and family. I was certainly taking care of our financial needs through my business, and I was there for my wife and kids; but what about me? A light bulb turned on.

I began to realize that there are three aspects to one's life. Most people have some type of a career—one side of the triangle: school, work, a full-time hobby, a volunteer position—something productive. Relationships form the second side of a triangle: spouse, parents, siblings, children, friends, business associates, interaction with other human beings. The third side is oneself, often the most neglected aspect of one's life. This is the component in the formula that is overlooked the most. I had rarely taken time just for myself. I was too busy expending parts of myself in my business and splitting myself even further between my wife and three children and their activities.

When you're juggling the career and relationship balls in the air, you need to add a third ball to the juggling act: yourself. It makes the juggling more difficult, but it is necessary. There's nothing wrong with paying attention to yourself. The challenge is balance. A lot of stress in people's lives is as a result of the imbalance between managing a career, relationships and taking care of oneself.

It is not uncommon to see young people today devoting so much time to their new careers after college. These newly graduated young adults are ready to conquer the world. Some spend eight to twelve hours a day at their new careers. Their relationships are neglected and they have no time for themselves.

Women today, on average, get married much later in life than they did forty years ago. They also have children much later. It was very common for us, in our baby furniture store, to see women in their mid- to late 30s coming in to shop during their first pregnancy, and we saw plenty of pregnant women in their early 40s. This was rare four decades ago. Today, careers trump family relationships and taking care of self-development. Starting a career can, in some cases, be the path to self-development. An excellent means of reaching that goal, as long as the efforts can be realized as self-development, and not blurred by simply a career move. It's the realizing of the changes and the growth in development that are as important as the changes themselves. As these men and women get older, their priorities become entrenched in their careers and relationships. But what about the individual? Where's the attention to one's own self?

The lack of attention to your own well-being begins to reveal harmful symptoms as careers and relationships cause more and more stress. When has this person devoted any time to developing more positive mental health? Where are the appropriate coping skills? The lack of attention to one's own psychological health shows up in the form of depression, alcoholism, drug addiction, divorce, abuse, or simply discontent and unhappiness.

In today's world, stress is compounded by technology. People are so inundated with information and the desire to stay connected, that the end result is not an increase in satisfaction and contentment but rather heightened frustration, pressure, and anxiety. Everywhere you look, the perfect person or the perfect lifestyle is there for viewing on TV, radio, cell phones, iPads, iPods, computers, and video billboards. The "perfect" lifestyle, with all the "things" that go along with it, is in our face at every turn.

Today, for example, couples are exposed to so much information on child rearing, must-have products, and the need to be the "best parents" possible that simple common sense is swept aside. Gadgets and electronic messaging have replaced simple human contact. It is rare to see two people carrying on a conversation without one or both of them checking their cell phones. The time and energy expended to have the newest and best products and lifestyle leaves no room for self-development, which turns out to be the most important exercise you can engage in, as long as it is not at the expense of family.

During my run, I loved the days when I was in the middle of nowhere. There were no signs of civilization; no sounds, no billboards on the side of the road, no technology, nothing but beautiful scenery, a nice breeze, and silence.

On the occasions that this kind of setting presented itself, I would stop, do a slow 360 degree turn, take a deep breath, and think, "This is what life is really about. I have to be the luckiest person in the world to have this experience." The feeling of peace and contentment was overpowering. I was so fortunate that I was at a point in my life where my priorities could shift from the pleasures of raising my family and conducting business to now focusing on pleasures for myself and Sheryl. Until my Transamerica run, I was rarely in this kind of setting, nor was I in the frame of mind to even appreciate it if I had experienced it. It helped put into perspective the loss of our business and I realized that yes, we were in a very undesirable phase of our life, but we had the tools to work out of it. The moments of self-pity were replaced by a sense of confidence and gratification that we would have a new life ahead of us. The unknown became an interesting mystery that I knew we would solve down the road.

When standing in those civilization-free settings, I realized the true value of silence and natural beauty, and how good they made me feel. There were no distractions to diminish the moment. That's when it was most clear to me just how happy and content I was. It was the absence of so much that had become a part of my life. The silence was deafening.

PEACE AND SOLITUDE ON THE PLAINS OF NEW MEXICO.

The imbalance from attending only to one's career and relationships will show its negative effects eventually. The two-income family with children may have the nice house in the suburbs, important jobs and titles, daycare or a nanny for the kids, play dates, and weekly get-togethers with friends and neighbors, but what about a plan for each adult to be alone. I don't mean hanging out with the guys or girls, but actually alone—to think and relax and just be with oneself, or simply listen to oneself.

Personal development is what it says: personal. This is the time to be devoted to looking in the mirror, honestly, and deciding the really important things that matter in your life. It is not time to problem-solve about work, family, or the ills of the world. This is the time to dream and move thoughts away from the usual, routine matters that you replay day after day.

Daydreaming is entertaining. You can let your mind wander anywhere. Using your imagination and just thinking while you're running is enjoyable, relaxing, and extremely healthy. Creating your own little world to be whoever or whatever you want is a refreshing break from the constant need to come up with answers or solve problems. What a great feeling to escape from the hectic world we live in. Each person needs some time to walk out the back door and enter a world of peace and quiet. My run across the country was my escape from responsibility, hard work, and having to come up with all the answers.

Unfortunately, most people today find the need to take in information or expose themselves to outside stimulation in the form of TV, music, or technology. Self-entertainment in the form of thinking and dreaming is pretty uncommon. In fact, most people find it difficult to be alone, doing nothing, for even a brief period of time.

My greatest vacation pleasure is going to a secluded beach and just lying there feeling the breeze, relaxing in the calming effect of the ocean and the beautiful blue skies, with no interference. No books, no music; nothing. Now that the world is filled with technological stimulation, the real pleasure for me is in escaping from it.

Go into your bedroom, lie on the bed, and just close your eyes and relax with no external stimulation. Can you do it for half an hour? Most will find it very difficult. Doing nothing and feeling good and relaxed in the process is an acquired pleasure. People have a need to be productive, always doing something to occupy their time. The thought of doing nothing and actually enjoying it is a real turn-off to most. At the least, people want to listen to music, to stimulate their senses. What about stimulating the inner sense of one's Self with silence and thought? Try doing it while you run.

Runners normally listen to music. Technology has made it so simple to stay plugged in to one's music of choice. If you ask runners why they listen to music, most will say it helps to pass the time and it prevents boredom. I found very early in my running that I could get so deeply involved in whatever I was thinking that I could run for miles without even paying attention to the running. It was as if I "woke up" and realized that I was miles and miles down the road. I was running on autopilot and didn't even feel the physical experience of running. That's when I realized that what I was doing and thinking about was much more of a boredom-buster than any amount of music I could have listened to.

So, running for me became an easy exercise of moving and creating and playing movies in my head for hours. It is the creating of a movie, fine-tuning it, and playing it over and over that makes my running so easy and enjoyable and devoid of boredom.

Exactly what you choose to think about may be different, but the principle remains. The reason I got so much pleasure out of this run across the country was that it afforded me much time to be totally alone; to do nothing but think my own thoughts and dream. Cell phones and computers were replaced by silence.

You may also discover that all this alone time to think and dream will lead to something that is in decline these days: common sense. With the influx of all the information we get from a multitude of sources, does one ever take the time to engage in some critical thinking? I came to realize that a lot of what I saw or heard, after a little thought, just didn't make sense. Do you stop to mull over the reasonableness of the plethora of sound bites you are subjected to? What is the motive of the source? What is the hidden agenda? I think you will find that the greater the volume of information, the greater the need to use common sense in analyzing its credibility. I spent hours while running, playing over and over, the purpose of diet commercials in my head. Special pills, supplements, and meals are sold in the billions. I wondered why the concept of self-control and discipline and exercise never seems to be the major part of the program. I guess it's easier to maintain inappropriate eating habits and take a magic pill, than to work on self-control and change the way one views his or her habits. For most people, exercise is a great idea, and buying all the sharp looking clothes is fun, but the interest wears off and old habits prevail.

Toward the end of my run, at the Imperial Sand Dunes in Glamis, California, I ran through miles and miles of nothing but sand and blue skies. The town of Glamis has a population of six. Except for the road I ran on, it was all beautiful sand dunes and nothing else. It was spectacular and quiet and hot — 114 degrees. I felt like I had opened the door to a huge furnace and climbed in.

I thought about my days in the Boston winters, got a little shiver, and then felt good, cooling off a bit. What a setting! A police car passed me and then turned around and stopped near me. The policeman asked if I was okay. I guess there weren't many runners in the area in the middle of summer.

When was the last time you were alone and listened to the silence of a natural setting? And enjoyed the moment? Most people find it hard.

Being out in a public place with a friend or family member is much more comfortable than being alone. If people find themselves alone, they may feel lonely or isolated. Being alone with nothing to do can be a very uncomfortable feeling for a lot of people. Try sitting in a doctor's office without an iPod or book. Try taking in your surroundings and relaxing. You may find that it is enjoyable and gives your mind a little time to unwind.

Although it's true that humans are social animals, don't let that conceal the positive qualities of wanting to spend time alone with your thoughts. Taking care of yourself by learning to embrace being alone to think and daydream enhances contentment and improves psychological strength and mental health. Being bombarded by outside sources satisfies the senses and triggers the act of interpretation, but it does little to formulate self-reflection, fantasies, dreams, or original ideas.

Growing as an individual is not a selfish exercise. In the long run, of the three components — career, relationships, and personal development — looking after your mental health is of the utmost importance. If you had to choose to focus all your attention on only one of the three aspects of your life, choosing to concentrate on your own psychological well-being would be the most practical and the healthiest choice. Would it be a selfish choice? Not at all. Fortunately, you don't have to choose only one.

When a person has addressed his own issues, made changes, can feel content and at peace with himself, has accepted responsibility for his own behavior, and is able to laugh at himself, then he can efficiently and effectively address his relationships and be more productive in his career.

In a relationship, if you want the other person to change his or her behavior, change your own instead; that, you have control over. Accept the fact that you don't have control over others. Don't expect them to change their behavior for your benefit. Trying to change someone else's behavior is an act of futility. Work on yourself. Once you have mastered yourself, you have the strength, confidence, and coping skills to navigate your daily interactions and workload, with or without changes in others. You may find that your tolerance and patience for others will increase.

Don't think that having the perfect relationship will lead to a better you or improve your performance at work. You may be riding an incredible "relationship high," but it may be a short-lived experience. What happens if the relationship sours? You become the tail being wagged by the dog. Where's the control on your part? Your well-being is subject to the whims of another. Enter a relationship on your terms, with empathy, flexibility, understanding, and a sense of humor. If it doesn't work out as expected, have the psychological strength to move on without diminishing your value as a person. One's self-worth should never be tied to the success or failure of a relationship, or one's career status.

The worst component of the formula to focus all your attention on is your career. Relationships and your own well-being will suffer and deteriorate. After a while you will feel the effects of your loneliness and discontent. Tying your self-image to your power, authority, job, title, or position is a sign of someone who needs the flashing billboard that lets the world know he is an important person. It will grow old for you and others after a while.

Attending to oneself is very important. Navigating life's daily challenges with self-confidence, contentment, and a strong sense of self gives you healthy and appropriate skills to enjoy life and suitably cope with the certain bumps in the road.

Careers come and go and relationships come and go. You are stuck with yourself, so why not devote the time and energy to feeling good and developing the healthy coping skills to address the daily stressors that surely come along.

My good friend Ric is a unique individual. He graduated from Harvard and then went to law school at UCal Berkley. After graduating, he began practicing in the law firm I used in Atlanta. He practiced for a few years, travelled for a while, then worked for the United Nations in its Vienna, Austria, office. After a number of years at the UN, he began living at an ashram in Kullu, India.

I mention my good friend because he realized very early on that, although the world could have been at his feet and he could have had what we might describe as the perfect life, he chose to devote his life to working on himself. Handsome, a brilliant attorney, and the nicest guy in the world—what else could one ask for? Ric forwent the wealth and beautiful lifestyle most only dream about and decided instead to study and learn in the ashram. He is the happiest and most content and fulfilled person I know. I see him every five years or so. We correspond by mail in the interim. No email, no text, no phone calls, except a weekly visit every five years. Observing, over a 30-year period, my friend's contentment and ability to enjoy life and keep things in perspective gave me much to think about.

Colleges teach subject matter to prepare the student for a career. Social networks and dating services match people by certain qualities and create a forum for people to meet and interact with each other. What about the individual and personal growth and attention to contentment? In our society, the most important aspect of this triangle is ignored. It is the individual's well-being that is the foundation that allows a person to enter a healthy relationship and become a productive member of society.

Too many people ignore the most important aspect of life. Is it a wonder that our society is filled with people who are depressed and lacking in healthy coping skills?

To avoid the pain and effort to improve oneself, people take the easy way out by masking their discomfort and resorting to unhealthy means of coping. Masking the pain is today's norm.

Blaming others for a life of unhappiness and lack of purpose is common. Wanting to move to a different city or find a new job is what people view as a solution to their discontent. You can't run away or hide from yourself. The first place to begin to get more out of life is by looking in the mirror—at yourself.

It takes quite a bit of work to balance careers, relationships, and personal growth. But it is doable and, oh does it feel good when everything is in balance.

CHAPTER **10** TEN

May I Pray with You?

I had a lot of firsts on my journey across the U.S. By the end, I can truthfully say that there was not much that surprised me.

While I was running just west of Monticello, Florida, a car stopped beside me and a woman rolled her passenger window down and asked me if she could pray with me. I was so stunned that I was silent for a moment. I thanked her and told her that I didn't think so today. She smiled and told me to have a blessed day and drove away.

As I continued my run I thought about the encounter and how strange it was for me. Not because I'm Jewish and have never really been exposed to this kind of offer, but that it was so foreign to me and how I reacted. Was this woman trying to help me be a better Christian? Or did she see me as someone in need and was offering comfort with prayer? I don't know. But I realized that it was an exchange that I was unable to relate to. Did she feel it her mission in life to improve people's lives with prayer, or did she genuinely feel that she was helping someone in need? Or did she want someone to pray with her, for her own benefit. Although I was running on the side of a country road, I didn't think I had the appearance of a person whose soul was lost. She may have thought that all people could use a little G-d time.

I then had some insight into the reaction of people whom we had told of my run across the country; an act, to them, that was just as bizarre as what I had just witnessed. For most people, the idea of running 20 miles a day for 2350 miles is incomprehensible. To me it was, or had become, something of an enjoyable daily routine, just checking out the scenery and weather in a new setting, for 20 miles down the road.

One of the results of this trip was that my sympathy and empathy for others increased. I saw that for me, running is an activity that I am comfortable with and fully understand. For this woman, her desire to bring another person closer to her G-d was what her world was about. Although it was not something I was interested in, I later appreciated and respected her efforts. Tolerance, patience, and acceptance were qualities that I acquired along the way. I'm grateful that over the course of the 119 days I was running, I found myself becoming much more open and tolerant with others' points of view.

Initially, from habit, my first response to this woman was one of surprise and disdain—another religious fanatic trying to cure the world with her religion. Someone seeing me running could have simply said, "What is this guy doing running across the country? He's 60 years old and he should be looking for a job."

This woman was as comfortable with her mission as I was with mine. We both had our dreams and goals that didn't necessarily conform to the norm. What mattered was that our dreams had value to each of us.

If I had it to do over again, I would take a few minutes to talk with the woman and compliment her on wanting to help a stranger; that act alone was worthy of a few minutes of my time and a heartfelt thank you. Time—I had had plenty of it. But I had missed the opportunity.

With my heightened attention to respect and courtesies towards others, I became much more aware of little things along the way, realizing that my generation and the one before mine enjoyed technology to a point.

As I passed through a very small town somewhere in Louisiana or Texas, I stopped at a small general store to get a drink. As I was waiting in line to pay, I noticed at the old-fashioned, manual cash register, a handwritten sign on a piece of cardboard that said. "I will be more than happy to wait on you, as soon as you get off your cell phone." I smiled as I read it, thinking of all the customers who came into our store and wandered around, talking on their phones. As I paid, I said to the elderly owner, "I like your sign," pointing to it. He looked at me and just shook his head. I knew exactly what he was thinking.

Coping Skills—The Bridges

As I approached the Cochrane-Africatown USA Bridge in Mobile, Alabama, I stopped and stared. It was high, about 140 feet above the Mobile River; it was about a mile and a half long. I was face to face with my biggest fear.

In fact, I was paralyzed with fear. I have moderate acrophobia, the fear of heights. Standing in high open places, rooftops, and balconies, scares me and makes my knees weak. On the occasions that I find myself unable to gracefully avoid having

COCHRANE-AFRICATOWN USA BRIDGE.

to be in such a situation—like at a friend's apartment on the thirtieth floor—I stay as far away from the edge as possible. I have gotten very adept at stretching my neck and making all the appropriate sounds of appreciation for the magnificent view, while privately trying to keep my knees from buckling.

How was I going to run across this bridge when I was so afraid that I couldn't move? I reached for my cell phone to call Sheryl. I asked her why she hadn't told me about the bridge. She had to have driven over it after she dropped me off. She said she didn't want to worry me. She had a point.

I started looking for another way to continue my westward trek but soon realized this was the path I had to travel if I wanted to get to San Diego. The number one priority, at this point in my life, was to hug my daughter while standing in the Pacific Ocean. I decided that I was going to cross the bridge even if it took hours and meant crawling on my hands and knees.

Taking a deep breath, with my heart in my throat, I started across; up the long, gradually inclining road. I slowed my pace and looked at a point immediately in front of my feet, glancing up to my right every few steps to check the oncoming traffic and resisting the urge to look over the edge to my left.

I was moving against traffic, on the left side of the road, and noticed the bridge had a slight tilt down to the left. This increased my anxiety and added to my fear. There was a guardrail, but I found myself running closer to the traffic than to it. This is contrary to what I normally do on roads. I try to run as far over on the shoulder, as far away from traffic as I can get. I was so terrified of the height and of getting too close to the edge, that I decided I'd rather get hit by a car or truck than fall 140 feet.

I kept looking just in front of my feet and tried to be aware of the cars to my right. After a few minutes, I saw three teenagers ahead of me. They were all wearing matching shirts, walking for some cause. I was too scared to even try to read what their shirts said. They were having the time of their lives talking, laughing, and bouncing with each step as though they were walking down Fifth Avenue. They were as close to the railing as you could get. I looked at them briefly and said to myself, "Are you kidding me? Don't get so close to the edge." They were enjoying this jaunt across the bridge, and I was almost having a panic attack!

Watching them so close to the edge made my knees weak. I finally passed them. Afraid to wave, I just nodded my head as I passed and continued to look down at my feet.

Shortly after leaving them behind, I crested the crown of the bridge and realized that I was halfway across. My satisfaction was brief because I knew I had over a half mile to go. The fact that I was descending didn't make me feel any better either. The slant of the bridge gave a pedestrian a very clear view of the ground. I felt compelled to glance over the side of the bridge to the earth far below a few times just to confirm why I was so scared. Mostly I kept my eyes down and toward the inside, glancing at the cars and trucks as they passed.

The bridge makes a huge curve to the left on the descent, and I kept running, picking up speed to shorten the time because I was in such a panic. As I started the gradual curve to the left, I could see that the height was lessening. I could see and feel the end in sight. By the time the bridge straightened out I was almost sprinting.

I ran off the bridge and slowed to a walk to catch my breath. The terror was over and I felt a huge sense of relief and an immediate drop in anxiety. I had done it.

ANOTHER HIGH BRIDGE, THIS ONE LEADING INTO KROTZ SPRINGS, LOUISIANA.

Was the fear real or exaggerated? Crossing the bridge did have some safety issues, but the terror I felt was amplified. I knew I was inflating the danger, which was how I conquered my fear enough to manage the crossing. I recognized the difference between real danger and danger created by me, in my mind.

My fear of heights is only in situations where I am exposed to open areas higher than 20 feet, about the height of a two-story building. As a kid, I loved to climb on the roof of our house and jump off. I was also a pole vaulter in high school, so I am well aware of just how irrational and illogical this fear is.

Being exposed on the top of tall buildings and high bridges is what makes me so uncomfortable and fearful. I've managed this irrational fear by looking at it rationally, and I've never allowed it to interfere with my daily life. Although I crossed many bridges on my run across the country, the Cochrane-Africatown USA Bridge in Mobile was certainly the most frightening.

Before I put one foot on any bridge, I stopped, looked at it, and decided the best way to navigate over it. Bridges with very little traffic were easier. I simply ran down the center of the lane, so I was unable to see over the edges. Since I was running against traffic, when I saw a car approach, I had time to run over to the shoulder and then go back to the center of the oncoming lane after the vehicle passed.

When I ran over the Morganza Spillway in Louisiana, there was no shoulder. I waved at traffic for the entire 1.8 miles, making sure everyone saw me. All but about five cars moved over to give me safe passage. It was scary, but manageable.

Fear can be managed if you think through the situation and override the emotional component that's causing the fear. If you're honest with yourself and acknowledge that you are fearful and, if you have the confidence, motivation, and desire to want something badly enough, you can address all of the daily challenges, large and small.

Since my top priority was to get to the west coast, I was motivated enough to think through the height issues and find a reasonable way to address each instance. Motivation was the key factor. There has to be a good enough reason and need for a fear to be addressed and bypassed. I decided early on that my motivation, my "picture on the wall," was hugging Julie as I stood in the Pacific. This was a simple thing, but it had a huge price tag on it.

Over the years, from my own experiences and observations, I saw a pattern of ways to mask pain and deal with uncomfortable situations. These selected responses became a habitual response in certain situations. I saw this in myself and noticed these responses in others. For myself, I realized that they were inappropriate behaviors and needed to be changed. In others, I simply recognized it and took note of my response and how it made me feel, being on the other end.

- Rationalizing—twisting facts to fit the scenario instead of facing the truth

- Blaming others

- Lying to cover up

- Kidding yourself (Telling yourself something is no big deal—when it actually is)

- Low impulse control—losing your temper

- Bullying

- Arrogance to mask insecurity

Some people will do just about anything to keep from accepting responsibility for their own actions. Some people take themselves so seriously that they cannot accept failure, will not admit when they are wrong, or simply can't apologize. They have built such a thick, protective coat of armor around their weak sense of self that they will resort to any mechanism to maintain that protection. And most importantly, they are unwilling to look in the mirror and engage in an honest appraisal of themselves.

A LITTLE SCARY, BUT THE VIEW WAS MAGNIFICENT IN MISSISSIPPI.

That's why it is so important to focus on your own well-being: so that the challenges in relationships, the workplace, and daily life can be appropriately dealt with.

In order for me to cross that Cochrane-Africatown USA Bridge in Mobile, a couple of things had to happen. First, I had to face the fear and, if not overcome it, at least manage to relegate it to a lesser place than my higher goal of reaching the Pacific. I saw this as another success, giving me more confidence to do it again and to overcome even bigger challenges as I moved west.

Second, I was able to laugh at the absurdity of how I exaggerated the danger. By viewing the situation from a different perspective, I adjusted down the intensity of my fear. I was very afraid while crossing the bridge but I knew I wasn't going to jump off or be pushed off, two of the strong feelings I have when I'm at a height of more than two stories. Was I really going to get too close to the traffic? I was fearful, but I'm not irrational, reckless, or careless.

There are many ways to view the same situation. If you can expand your thinking process to allow for a shift in views, you can select the vantage point that best allows for the appropriate action. From experience, I realized that when I approached those bridges and spillways, I just had to give my imagination free rein, experience the fear, be irrational for a while, and then get down to the business at hand and deal with it in a rational manner. As I reached for my phone to call Sheryl at that first bridge in Mobile, I already knew I was going to run over it. I just needed some time to go through the processing and get mentally readjusted to cross.

The Nike slogan, "Just Do It" is great. At some point, you just have to quit the procrastinating, quit the analyzing, quit the fidgeting, quit giving excuses, and just do it. The more you push yourself through your fears, the more confidence and less hesitation you'll have the next time. Fear is debilitating and if you are unable to shift perspective, you will have more anxiety and stress, take less action, and implement more avoidance. Unless you address your inability to cope, avoidance behavior gets stronger. For example, it's much easier to reach for a bottle of liquor than to confront an unhappy marriage or the loss of a job. The problem goes away after a few drinks. Or does it?

Developing healthy coping skills takes honesty, courage, and practice. It starts by taking a good hard look in the mirror. Stay focused on yourself go through the process by yourself without rushing to others for help. Self-reliance affords the opportunity to cope with issues on your own and will precipitate learning experiences for the next problem to draw from. It also builds self-confidence and gives one the psychological strength to repeat the process.

This is something that has to be done alone. It is a process that requires self-evaluation. It takes honesty and an acceptance that you may not be so strong and that you may not be the person you prefer the world to see, but you can now take the assets you do have and maximize them to bring about self-improvement. Change your view both of yourself and of yourself in relation to your surroundings.

As my running increased over the years, I had the time, desire, honesty, and motivation to consciously change. I took mental notes of what I was doing to bring about my changes and also noticed how it was making me feel. I saw that the breaking away from repetitive, automatic responses in certain situations was a conscious exercise that I had to force sometimes until it became more comfortable. And it paid off well.

As I ran, I thought. As I thought, I took a more realistic and honest approach to inappropriate habitual responses and noticed consciously planned strategies from a new vantage point:

- Be honest with yourself.

- Take an inventory of your good and bad qualities.

- Embrace your good qualities so you can enhance them.

- Laugh at yourself—don't take yourself so seriously. You're really not as important as you think you are. This is life changing—not life threatening.

- Learn to apologize. No harm in being wrong.

- Look at situations from different vantage points and make new, more appropriate decisions on how to respond.

- Consciously catch yourself making the same negative response to the same situation. Recognize your patterns and get out of the habit of same situation, same response.

- Before acting, take a few moments to pause and think of a new way to view the situation.

- Give yourself a reason to get motivated.

- Start with small changes, succeed, and feel good about it.

- With new confidence, incorporate healthy coping skills into your daily life, and consciously use them.

- Consciously ditch the unhealthy coping skills.

As I entered the western part of Texas, I was still running without carrying fluids or food with me. I didn't have a water belt or a Camelbak, which is a water backpack with a long, plastic tube to serve as a straw. I relied solely on running past convenience stores and stopping, or passing businesses, churches, or houses and asking for a drink or drinking out of an outside faucet. Runners are creatures of habit and I was used to running with the bare minimum—shirt, shorts, socks, shoes, and cell phone. I did make one concession: about a week after leaving Jacksonville Beach, I begin to wear a hat. Other things were added later in the run, as needed.

One day in west Texas, I ran 20 miles with nothing to eat or drink. At first I was concerned. It was a very hot day and I was very thirsty and dry. My lips were cracking from the heat and dryness. I realized that my days of buying fluids at convenience stores or sipping water from a faucet were over. I was able to stop and look at the situation from a logical, rational perspective.

Instead of looking at what my problems were (no water, no food, 10 miles to go, cracked lips, etc.), I decided to view this episode as simply poor planning (being honest with myself), and that I was really okay—very thirsty, very hot, very hungry, very tired, but okay. So, I continued the run and planned from the next day on to carry a water belt. I was lucky this time and I promised myself that it would not happen again.

I adapted to the conditions and felt good that I had the confidence to feel that, no matter what the obstacle, I'd just figure it out. I took the approach that, in some cases, I needed to be in survival mode, and I'd figure out what I had to do to make it through the run.

This was not an attitude or approach that developed during my run. This was a coping skill that allowed me to not only take the first steps away from the Atlantic Ocean on day one, but to manage each of the 119 days of running that followed—and to enjoy them.

In order to effectively cope with the daily bumps in life, large and small, one has to view oneself as the responsible party, with the free will to select appropriate or inappropriate behavior. Once you gain control over yourself, you will begin to have more fun on the journey of running as well as this journey through life.

Worry about yourself and your condition; not others. As I mentioned earlier, if you want to change someone else's behavior, first change your own. The best way to get rid of someone's inappropriate behavior is to ignore it. You will eventually find that the more you attend to yourself and grow more content with your life, the less impact others will have on you. You will begin to see that the annoying people who surrounded you before are simply part of the scenery that can be overlooked. You will no longer feel the emotional drain experienced while in the presence of certain people.

Family members, friends, and acquaintances whom you feel the need to sway to your way of thinking, argue with, or simply allow to get under your skin, will become a part of your landscape that you can glance at, nod, and then ignore. Proving a point will no longer be a necessity.

Coping comes from you—how you see a situation, interpret it, and respond. You're the one who chooses to engage in or ignore a situation. If you choose to engage and be part of a situation, appropriate coping skills will allow you to respond rather than to simply react emotionally and possibly inappropriately.

I dealt with losing my business and being unemployed by seeing it as an opportunity to fulfill a dream and start a new life. I had the confidence to see the positives and personal benefits, while refusing to let the negatives spoil a good adventure. The negatives far outweighed the positives from a practical perspective, but whoever said "practical" was fun and rewarding?

I also made sure that I wasn't kidding myself into thinking that a run across the country would cure our joblessness and homelessness. I was hoping, as an aside, that

I'd get some media exposure and someone would see the value in hiring either Sheryl or me. But I was fully prepared to face the task of finding work after the adventure concluded. I knew the run was simply a brief interlude before we had to address our financial situation and our future.

You can be well educated. You can be surrounded by the most loving of families, but if you haven't learned to cope with the everyday stressors of life with inner strength, confidence, courage, and a sense of humor, you are doomed to a life of being miserable while constantly putting out one fire after another.

The toll on a person who can't cope with daily stress is enormous, both physiologically and psychologically. It's like being swept up by a tornado and whipped around and slammed to the ground with each stressful situation.

CHAPTER **12** TWELVE

Food—Eat, Drink, and Be Happy

For five and a half months, I had the good fortune to be able to eat and drink whatever I wanted, and in whatever quantity I wanted. One could even make a convincing argument that I ran across the country just so I could partake in a six-month feed-a-thon. That wasn't the case, but I have to admit that 4,000 calories per day is a lot of good eating.

Under normal conditions, I'd skip breakfast, eat lunch around 1:00 p.m., and either have some or no dinner. My erratic and probably unhealthy eating routine was formed as a revolt against my rigid, three-square-meals-on-time every day routine growing up. I eat if I'm hungry and don't eat if I'm not. Sometimes I gorge myself, sometimes I starve myself. My eating behavior is as irregular as can be; three bowls of Cheerios and milk for dinner is fine with me. A doctor advising a long-distance runner might have different thoughts.

I know when I need to put on the brakes and I have the discipline to just stop eating. If I have to lose a few pounds, my diet is very simple: I eat one meal around 2:00-3:00 p.m. and that's it. I go to sleep hungry and wake up feeling lighter which gives me immediate positive feedback that I am, in fact, losing weight. I do this for about a week, and I'm back to my normal weight. Again, because I'm not a doctor and I don't play one on television, you should probably talk with a trained professional when deciding how to conduct your own diet.

When we began our trip to Jacksonville before the run, Sheryl loaded the car with cases of Gatorade, bananas, and bagels. I thought this would be a daily carb load, just like running marathons. I'd get up, get dressed, eat some bagels, drink a lot of Gatorade, have a few bananas, and I'd be off. But it made me feel heavy, which was not normal for me.

It finally dawned on me one day, running and feeling sluggish, that I wasn't running marathons. I was running 20 miles. I had never loaded up with carbs for a 20-mile training run. I usually got up, got dressed, took a few sips of water, and off I went. After my run that day, I told Sheryl I needed to stop treating these 20-mile runs as marathons.

I went back to my normal routine: I got up, got dressed, drank a Gatorade or ice water in the car driving to where I was going to start that day's run, and off I went. I either had money for a snack and drink, or I had my water belt or Camelbak. There was no need for pre-run loading.

But after my daily run, the feeding frenzy began. By the time I went to bed, I made sure I had consumed at least 4000 calories. I never actually calculated the calories I was eating; I just had a sense of when I was adequately fueled for the next day's run.

Depending on how hungry I was, or how much I had fixated on a particular meal while running, we'd stop at a fast-food place on the way back to the hotel, or I'd shower and dress and then go eat.

I NEEDED TO EAT AT LEAST 4000 CALORIES A DAY IN ORDER TO FUEL THE RUN. NOW THAT WAS FUN!

We usually either ate fast food, or made sandwiches in the hotel room for lunch and then went out for dinner. I'd get hot for a particular food, then after a week or so, move on to something else. First, it was Subway tuna sandwiches, Doritos, and a coke. I craved this combo for about ten days straight.

Then I got sick of that and moved on to Sonic—a No. 1 double burger all the way with no cheese, tots, and a cherry slush. Next came McDonald's.

One day I was running and I saw a billboard for its fish sandwiches. That's all I could think of for the rest of the run. When Sheryl picked me up, I told her we needed to go to McDonalds—immediately! She said, "What? You hate McDonalds!"

"I know, but I have to have some fish sandwiches and fries." So we ate at McDonalds for about a week.

In California, we finally stopped at our first Carl's Jr. in El Centro, California. It's like the western version of Hardees. This was a step-up fast-food place. They serve great hamburgers, the restaurant is clean, and the service is friendly.

CARB LOADING OVER PASSOVER IN HOUSTON, TEXAS.

At dinnertime on our trip, we'd look for the flavor of the local fare. We'd ask around and try to find restaurants or diners that had been around forever and that the locals frequented. We ate a lot of great dinners in amazing local restaurants. The people were friendly and accommodating and the food was really terrific. Throughout the entire run, dinner felt like our daily celebration of another successful day on the road.

A few meals stood out: A rib eye and baked potato dinner at Sweetie Pie's Ribeyes in Decatur, Texas; a steak dinner in Giddings, Texas, to celebrate the first 1000 miles; Cajun food at Fausto's in Kinder, Louisiana; the best fajitas at Leal's in Clovis, New Mexico; the best homemade fajitas at Jeff and Julia Baker's house in Albuquerque, New Mexico; the best Japanese food at Roka Akor in Scottsdale, Arizona, celebrating our fortieth anniversary; best hamburger and chocolate shake at Dairyland in Ft. Sumner, New Mexico; the best atmosphere and experience at The Café in Buffalo Gap, Texas.

Best historic diner of all? Joseph's, on historic Route 66 in Santa Rosa, New Mexico.

After getting the final load of my calorie quota, I'd look forward to returning to the hotel, getting into bed, watching some TV, and having a good night's sleep. I never had any pressure to wake up at a certain time. I let my body dictate how much sleep I needed and got up when I felt rested. It was usually around 6:30 in the morning. As we got farther west, I found I was waking up around 5:30. I'd never gotten up that early before, but I had gotten my seven to eight hours of sleep and was ready to begin my run for that day.

A VARIETY OF TERRAIN IN NEW MEXICO.

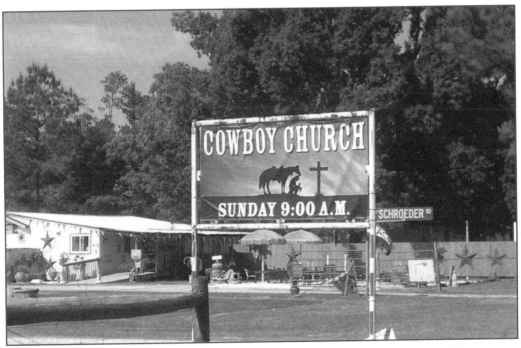

COULD NEVER FIGURE OUT EXACTLY WHAT A COWBOY CHURCH WAS—I PASSED QUITE A FEW IN TEXAS.

PALM TREES LINE THE ROAD TO EL CENTRO, CA. NICE CHANGE OF SCENERY.

RUNNING THROUGH PEARLINGTON, MISS. I SMELL A PATERNITY SUIT.

PROOFREADER FOR HIRE SOMEWHERE IN NEW MEXICO.

IF YOU THINK HE LOOKS BAD, YOU SHOULD SEE THE ALIEN SPACECRAFT THAT HIT HIM, SOMEWHERE IN NEW MEXICO.

ONLY NON-BRANDED HOTEL ON THE TRIP IN SPRINGERVILLE, ARIZ. TRYING TO ESCAPE THE SMOKE FROM THE WALLOW FIRE.

SMOKEY THE BEAR WAS THE MAN IN THIS PART OF ARIZONA.

ALL BUT ONE RATTLESNAKE I SAW WAS DEAD ON THE SIDE OF THE ROAD—FORTUNATELY!

FLAT, EASY RUNNING BEFORE I HIT THE MOUNTAINS JUST EAST OF SAN DIEGO.

VERY BAD DUST STORM ENTERING TAHOKA, TEXAS ON MAY 24, 2011.

I GOT WATER WHEREVER I COULD GET IT.

SHERYL THOUGHT WE WERE DONE WITH COIN-OP LAUNDROMATS WHEN WE FINISHED COLLEGE.

TONOPAH-SALOME HIGHWAY OUTSIDE PHOENIX. DOES THIS LOOK LIKE A HIGHWAY TO YOU? MAPS CAN BE DECEIVING!

SOMETIMES ENTERTAINMENT CAME IN THE FORM OF PROOFREADING.

OLD WEST TOWN IN ALBANY, TEXAS.

OUTSIDE THE DRISKILL HOTEL IN AUSTIN, TEXAS.

GENERAL STORE IN LEDBETTER, TEXAS. ESTABLISHED IN THE 1880'S.

LIMPING THROUGH OCEAN SPRINGS, MISSISSIPPI ON A BUM LEG.

THERE WERE FAR TOO MANY SAD MEMORIALS ALONG THE WAY.

RUNAWAY BAY IN TEXAS. A BEAUTIFUL RUN OVER THE BRIDGE.

I PASSED OVER THE BRAZOS RIVER IN TEXAS FOUR TIMES.

SIGN POSTED INSIDE THE BANK IN BUFFALO GAP HISTORIC VILLAGE, TEXAS.

THE BENEFITS OF RUNNING TOWARD TRAFFIC.

SHERYL AND I MET SO MANY INTERESTING PEOPLE ON OUR RUN ACROSS THE COUNTRY.

BEAUTIFUL SCENERY THROUGHOUT ARIZONA.

PASSING THE USS ALABAMA AS I ENTER MOBILE—ROLL TIDE!!

RUNNING OVER THE RIO GRANDE RIVER JUST OUTSIDE OF BELEN, NEW MEXICO.

THE MISSISSIPPI RIVER IN BATON ROUGE, LOUISIANA.

HARD TO BELIEVE. ONLY FIVE MORE RUNNING DAYS UNTIL I CROSS INTO TEXAS—STATE #5.

SNOWBALL STANDS THROUGHOUT LOUISIANA.

BEAUTIFUL WIDE OPEN SPACES NEAR POST, TEXAS, JUST BEFORE THE DUST STORM HIT.

RUNNING BY ESCAMBIA BAY OUTSIDE PENSACOLA, FLORIDA.

BEAUTIFUL WITCHWOOD HOUSE ON PERDIDO BAY.

BEAUTIFUL HOMES ALONG GOVERNMENT STREET IN MOBILE, ALABAMA.

ONE OF MANY HOMELESS TRAVELERS I PASSED ALONG THE WAY TO SAN DIEGO.

ENTERING BILOXI, MISSISSIPPI.

BEAUTIFUL BEACHES ALONG THE MISSISSIPPI GULF COAST, FRESH AND CLEAN AFTER KATRINA AND OTHER HURRICANES
SWEPT THE STRUCTURES AWAY.

AND THE STREET NUMBER IS???

BRIDGES AND ROADS IN LOUISIANA WERE NOT PEDESTRIAN FRIENDLY.

SOME OF THE SHOULDERS ON THE ROADS IN MISSISSIPPI AND LOUISIANA WERE VERY NARROW.

RUNNING INCLUDED HOPPING OVER RAILROAD TRACKS AND PASSING UNDER BRIDGES.

RUNNING THROUGH PORT BARRE, LOUISIANA. A STOP FOR A DRINK AT A BIKER BAR.

BEAUTIFUL HISTORIC HOME IN LAWTELL, LOUISIANA.

LOCAL RESTAURANT IN KINDER, LOUISIANA. AMAZING CAJUN FOOD.

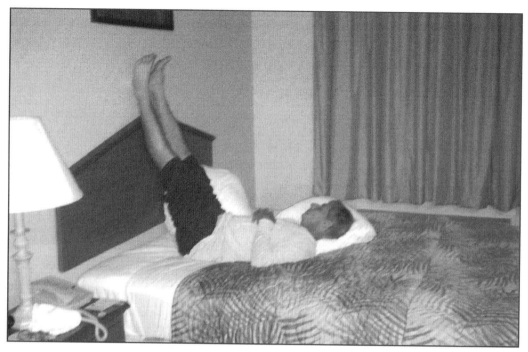

THE CURE FOR SWOLLEN FEET AND ANKLES.

BEAUTIFUL MURALS THROUGHOUT DEQUINCY, LOUISIANA, HOME OF THE STATE RAILROAD MUSEUM.

ENTERING THE STATE OF TEXAS—STATE #5.

THANK GOODNESS!!

A TEXAS WATER FOUNTAIN.

SO MANY HUGE ESTATES AND RANCHES IN TEXAS.

A STOP FOR WATER AND MAKING A NEW FRIEND.

LONE STAR ISLAND NEAR CUT AND SHOOT, TEXAS.

LUKES RUNNING STORE IN THE WOODLANDS, JUST NORTH OF HOUSTON. THANKS LADIES FOR ALL THE HELP AND ADVISE.

NICE MELONS NORTH OF HOUSTON.

MONTGOMERY, TEXAS.

GIDDINGS, TEXAS— DAY 50. 1000 MILES RUN, 1350 MILES TO GO.

MILES TO GO BEFORE I SLEEP.

HISTORIC DRISKILL HOTEL IN AUSTIN, TEXAS.

TEXAS/OKLAHOMA BASEBALL GAME ON THE UNIVERSITY OF TEXAS CAMPUS. BEAUTIFUL!

JACK COUNTY—BIRTHPLACE OF THE 4-H CLUB.

SMALL TOWN SPRING FAIR IN GRAHAM, TEXAS.

ANOTHER WIDE LOAD TO AVOID IN TEXAS.

BEAUTIFUL FARMLAND IN TEXAS.

NO GOOD DEED GOES UNPUNISHED. HE PEED ON ME AS I PICKED HIM UP OFF THE ROAD.

CHAPTER  THIRTEEN

The Eight States

There were two distinct and different parts of my run. East of Lubbock, Texas, was more densely populated. Motels were easier to find. I was able to run without needing to carry food or water. There were plenty of stores, houses, businesses, and churches from which to get water and food if necessary.

West of Lubbock was a different story. Towns were sometimes 30 to 40 miles apart. There was rarely a house or church or store in the middle of nowhere that I could stop to get water. I had to carry my own. The compensating factor was that the scenery was magnificent and so different from east of Lubbock.

I didn't actually run through Lubbock, but we stayed there and made it our base to run in more isolated areas where there were no accommodations.

The cities I ran through ranged in size from a population of six, in Glamis, California, and Yeso, New Mexico, to our regular big U.S. cities such as Jacksonville, Mobile, Baton Rouge, and Phoenix. I loved running through the smaller ones best; they are what America is all about. A lot of these smaller cities are hurting badly from years of decay and poor economies. They have their own distinctive styles of architecture, landscapes, vegetation, and animals.

Sheryl and I met a lot of wonderful, down-to-earth, hardworking or unemployed Americans along the way; really nice people. We met them in restaurants, stores, on the road, in parks. They had different accents, clothes, and customs.

The panhandle of Florida had beautiful beaches, poor small towns, rednecks, neat town squares, great southern cooking, friendly people, and cheaper gas.

Alabama, where I grew up, had childhood friends to visit; childhood beaches to see; the USS Alabama; University of Alabama fans and memorabilia everywhere; the Cochrane-Africatown USA Bridge that terrorized me; The Road Kill Café; rude Auburn fans; beautiful southern mansions; and lush green pastureland.

Mississippi had new, beautiful, unspoiled beaches, great seafood, and the best new bridges to run across.

Louisiana had snowballs, Cajun food, Cajun accents, and poor road and bridge running conditions.

Texas was huge, with cowboys, cowgirls, horses, cattle, no water, Lone Stars on houses, Texas flags in front yards, rodeos, chuck wagons, beautiful farm lands, and a lot of wide-open spaces, wind turbines, and very friendly people.

New Mexico had strong winds, mountains, red and green peppers, great Mexican food, friendly Mexicans and Native Americans, Route 66, smoke from Arizona wildfires, the VLA (Very Large Array, one of the world's premier astronomical radio observatories), mountains, the Continental Divide, pies, a lot of wide-open spaces, and the Blue Hole.

Arizona had mountains and valleys, cooler temps in the mountain areas and the hottest temps in the valley, forest fires, Tonto National Forest, The Wigwam, few roads to run on, interstate running, border patrols, twin cities (Pinetop/Lakeside, Heber/Overgaard), odd names of towns, copper mining, huge 4th of July celebrations, our fortieth anniversary celebration, and relaxing pools.

California had intense heat, desert, sand dunes, mountains, dips in the road, farming, irrigation systems, palm trees, expensive gas, few east-west roads, In-N-Out Burgers, beautiful beaches, surfing, Julie, and the Pacific Ocean.

CHAPTER **14** FOURTEEN

The 272

Here are the 272 cities and towns which I ran through. Thank you to all the folks in these places who extended themselves for Sheryl and me.

ANOTHER RECONNECTION FROM CHILDHOOD. JUDGE MARY IN MAGNOLIA SPRINGS, ALABAMA. PROUD OWNER OF HAUNTED WITCHWOOD.

FLORIDA (67): Jacksonville Beach, Jacksonville, Whitehouse, Halsema, Otis, Baldwin, Mattox, Mcclenny, Glen St. Mary, Pine Top, Margaretta, Sanderson, Manns Spur, Olustee, Mt. Carrie, Lake City, Houston, Live Oak, Dickert, Falmouth, Ellaville, Lee, West Farm, Madison, Greenville, Monticello, Montivilla, Baum, Black Creek, Lafayette, Tallahassee, Ochlocknee, Midway, Quincy, Gretna, Mt. Pleasant, Oak Grove, Chattahoochee, Sneads, Grand Ridge, Cypress, Marianna, Chipley, Hulaw, Bonifay, Caryville, Westville, Ponce De Leon, Argyle, Koerber, DeFuniak Springs, Santa Rosa Beach, San Destin, Miramar Beach, Destin, Ft. Walton Beach, Mary Ester, Wynnhaven Beach, Navarre, Harold, Milton, Pace, Riverview, Yniestra, Bohemia, Gaberonne, Pensacola.

STATELY MANSION ALONG GOVERNMENT STREET IN MOBILE, ALABAMA.

ALABAMA (17): Beulah, Seminole, Elsanor, Elberta, Foley, Magnolia Springs, Yupon, Turkey Branch, Barnwell, Magazine, Mobile, Tillman's Corner, Theodore, Irvington, St. Elmo, Fernland, Grand Bay.

MISSISSIPPI (13): Pecan, Orange Grove, Pascagoula, Gautier, Ocean Springs, Biloxi, Gulf Port, Long Beach, Pass Christian, Henderson Point, Bay St. Louis, Waveland, Pearlington.

BEAUTIFUL HOME ALONG THE GULF RUN THROUGH PASS CHRISTIAN, MISSISSIPPI.

HEADING TO BAY ST. LOUIS. A LOT OF BRIDGES IN MISSISSIPPI WERE REBUILT AFTER KATRINA AND OTHER HURRICANES.

LOUISIANA (48): Slidell, Lacombe, Mandeville, Covington, Goodbee, Robert, Coburn, Hammond, Woodhaven, Holden, Livingston, Satsuma, Walker, Dedham Springs, Castlewood, Baton Rouge, Lobdell, Carey, Erwinville, Lavonia, Blanks, Lottie, Krotz Springs, Courtableau, Hazelwood, Port Barre, Opelousas, Lawtell, Swords, Eunice, Tyrone, Basille, Barnsdall, Coverdale, Lauderdale, Kinder, Stanley, Le Blanc, Reeves, Bel, Fulton, Kernan, Gordon, Ragley, De Quincy, Lucas, Lunita, Starks.

TEXAS (50): Deweyville, Mauriceville, Vidor, Rose City, Beaumont, Bevil, Oaks, Sour Lake, Batson, Moss Hill, Cleveland, Fostoria, Security, Midway, Cut and Shoot, Conroe, Montgomery, Dobbin, Plantersville, Stoneham, Navasota, Earlywine, Brenham, Burton, Carmine, Ledbetter, Giddings, Hills, Runaway Bay, Vineyard, Jacksboro, Senate, Bryson, Graham, Breckenridge, Albany, Funston, Anson, Roby, Snyder, Gail, Tahoka, West Point, Brownfield, Gomez, Tokio, Plains, Progress, Lariat, Farwell.

NEW MEXICO (32): Texico, Clovis, Portair, Cannon Air Force Base, Grier, St. Vrain, Melrose, Krider, La Lande, Tolar, Taiban, Ft. Sumner, Yeso, Largo, Vaughn, Tejon, Carnero, Encino, Culebra, Lucy, Silio, Willard, Mountainaire, Abo, Scholle, Bernardo, Socorro, Magdalena, Datil, Pie Town, Quemado, Red Hill.

ROADKILL CAFÉ IN ELBERTA, ALABAMA. KILLER LUNCH BUFFET—ROLL TIDE!

ARIZONA (27): Springerville, Green Spot, Vernon, Bell, Show Low, Linden, Clay Springs, Overgaard, Heber, Forest Lakes, Globe, Superior, Florence Junction, Apache Junction, Navaho Station, Gold Canyon, Mesa, Phoenix, Litchfield Park, Goodyear, Perryville, Liberty, Buckeye, Tonopah, Quartzite, Ehrenberg.

CALIFORNIA (18): East Blyth, Blyth, Ripley, Palo Verde, Glamis, Brawley, Westmoreland, Elmore

WITH A NAME LIKE SWEETIE PIE'S, IT HAD TO BE GOOD. IT WAS, AND WE HAD AN AWESOME DINNER IN DECATUR, TEXAS.

Desert Ranch, Kane Spring, Ocotillo Wells, Banner, Julian, Wynola, Santa Ysabel, Witch Creek, Romona, Poway, Pacific Beach.

The many examples of Americana along the way let me know that, despite differences in local color between and within states, we are indeed one country from sea to shining sea. Here are the most prevalent establishments and sightings throughout the run, in big and small towns: Walmart, Dollar General, bail bonds, auto repair shops, auto parts shops, churches (Methodist and Baptist), For Sale signs, empty storefronts, Sonic Drive-ins, and McDonalds.

Road kill varied in kind and quantity by state:

- Florida: possum, squirrels (huge numbers)
- Alabama: possum, squirrels (huge numbers)
- Mississippi: possum, squirrels (huge numbers)
- Louisiana: possum, armadillos (in the west) (a lot)
- Texas: armadillos, cattle, rattlesnakes (some)
- New Mexico: cattle, deer (some)
- Arizona: not much road kill at all
- California: not much road kill at all

It's hard to say which town or city I liked best, but here is a brief mention of a few places that stood out and why.

Jacksonville Beach: It wasn't until I checked into the location where I would begin my run that I realized I would actually be starting about 18 miles east of the City of Jacksonville. The beach was beautiful—the start of my run at sunrise was a fitting beginning on Valentine's Day 2011.

Monticello, Florida—Monticello has a beautiful courthouse that borders the town square, and along Route 90 are turn-of-the-century houses in immaculate condition. This was the town where the kind lady stopped to ask me if she could pray with me. We had a great lunch at the Sage Restaurant. The owner was from Atlanta and happened to have been a cook at our favorite restaurant in the Virginia-Highland area—Fontaine's Oyster House.

Tallahassee, Florida—As I approached the city of Tallahassee, there was quite a bit of construction going on. I had to jump over the concrete barriers and run through dirt and just-paved sections of road. I also got to run on the main street that fronts Florida State University and see the Florida capitol up close. The FSU campus is beautiful.

DeFuniak Springs, Florida—DeFuniak Springs is another quaint town with a beautiful, historic town center. I remembered this by name only as one of the places our family passed through traveling from Montgomery on our way to the Gulf Coast for family summer vacations when I was a child.

Sandestin, Florida—Sandestin was the beach town where Sheryl and I spent our summer vacations starting in 1999. I ran over the exact route I used to run in the mornings each day on our vacations before we hit the beach. It has great restaurants, great little shops for Sheryl, and one of the prettiest beaches in the world. Many a day, I would lie on that beach from 10:00 a.m. until 4:00 p.m. The breeze, the sun, the pure white sand, and blue-green water...a wonderfully relaxing time for us. We loved the all-you-can-eat crab leg dinners at Elmo's Grill on County Highway 30A.

We were able to stay with my good friend Alan and his wife, Lisa, while in the area. He has a home in Watercolor Inn and Resort. Alan is a tri-athlete and rode his bike alongside me for about eight miles on my only day of rain of the entire trip. The heavens opened up as he began his ride back over the bridge from Ft. Walton Beach to Destin. He was lucky to be picked up by a guy passing in his pickup truck and made it back safely. My day ended at a porn shop (See Chapter 16).

Ft. Walton Beach, Florida—Ft. Walton Beach was another destination area, along with Panama City, for some of our family vacations when I was growing up. It's another part of the "Redneck Riviera" that has pure white sand that crunches when you walk on it. It has amazing seafood restaurants and was a great place to be a kid on summer vacation.

ONE OF MANY BEAUTIFUL HOMES ALONG SCENIC ROUTE 90 ON ESCAMBIA BAY JUST OUTSIDE OF PENSACOLA, FLORIDA.

Pensacola, Florida—I took the scenic U.S. Highway 90 route just by luck. I had come to a fork in the road and decided to take the route along Escambia Bay. I had no idea that I would be passing such beautiful homes that lined the bay.

Elberta, Foley, and Magnolia Springs, Alabama—These three towns are side by side along U.S. Highway 98 in LA (Lower Alabama). While running in this area we were able to stay with my childhood friend, Mary, at Witchwood House on Perdido Bay. It's a frightening haunted house (in my estimation). Actually, we bypassed the main house and stayed in Victoria, a smaller house adjacent to Witchwood. These three towns are thriving and alive, something I didn't see very often in small towns. We actually got gas at a station that allows you to pump before you pay. When was the last time you experienced that?

Mobile, Alabama—This is where I ran over the Cochrane-Africatown USA Bridge. One hundred forty feet above the ground, tilted toward the outside edge, and about a mile and a half long. I'll never forget the grip of pure terror as I ran and shuffled along, staying closer to the heavy traffic than to the shoulder overlooking the falloff. Magnificent homes lined parts of Government Street, the road I travelled as I ran through Mobile toward the Mississippi line.

MAGNIFICENT SUNSET OVER BILOXI, MISSISSIPPI.

Biloxi, Gulf Port, Long Beach, and Pass Christian, Mississippi— When I crossed the beautiful new bridge leading into Biloxi, I saw the Beau Rivage Hotel and Casino to my left. They were very nice, small-scale versions of their counterparts in Las Vegas.

I was amazed at the beauty of the beaches in the area and how open and uncluttered they were. I realized that the honky-tonk atmosphere of a typical beach town was not evident here because it had been washed clean by Katrina. What remained was the natural beauty of a pristine beach area. The water wasn't as pretty as the Florida or Alabama waters, but the beach was clean, almost desert-like, and very quiet. It was an area still recovering from the destruction of the hurricanes.

I also ran past Jefferson Davis' beautiful mansion, across the street from the beach. There is nothing like running along the beach in beautiful weather with a mild ocean breeze blowing over your body.

Pearlington, Mississippi—I will never forget Pearlington, a little, unkempt town I came to just as I was leaving Mississippi and crossing a small bridge into Louisiana. It was just before I got to the town that I ran more than a mile in the wrong direction. Between my not paying close attention and poorly marked road signs, I went a long way off course. This was when my leg was really hurting and I was angry and frustrated that, on top of the pain, I had gotten misdirected and had to backtrack.

I finally got back on the right road and headed into the residential area of Pearlington. A pack of dogs came running after me as a man stood and watched. It was the first of three times I had to use my mace on angry dogs. I hated to use it, but I was afraid of getting bitten. The man did nothing. The mace worked, and I was able to get out of the area with all body parts intact.

I stopped and got a drink from an outside vending machine at a volunteer fire station. Then I crossed the bridge leading into Louisiana and got my first taste of the poor roads and running conditions of the state. The bridge had no shoulder so I had to sprint across and hop up onto the railing as cars passed. This was not my idea of a fun run, but I made it and crossed into my fourth state.

THE ONLY RUNNER I CAME ACROSS. WE RAN TOGETHER FOR A FEW MILES AND HAD LUNCH ON OUR TRIP BACK EAST.

Covington, Louisiana—As I ran on the outskirts of Covington, another runner came up beside me and we began to talk as we ran. Michael is a local doctor. We ran together for about five miles. I told him about my run and we spoke about Louisiana politics and other things related to his state. It was great conversation.

When I got back to the hotel, I told Sheryl about my brief running partner. A few minutes later she looked at her cell phone and told me Michael had just made a very substantial donation to our run. I was shocked that a total stranger would be so kind and generous. My faith in humans was slowly beginning to be revived.

On our return trip back east, we met Michael at the local Covington Hospital for lunch. A prince of a guy.

Baton Rouge, Louisiana (Red Stick)—I met up with a woman I had grown up with in Montgomery. I hadn't seen Rhea and her husband, Raymond, in more than forty years. Despite my boundless allegiance to the University of Alabama, I have to say that the LSU campus, where Raymond is a professor, is beautiful. We ate breakfast together on campus.

THE I-10 BRIDGE OVER THE MISSISSIPPI RIVER IN BATON ROUGE, LOUISIANA.

I had a problem crossing the Mississippi River here. The road I was on, going through Baton Rouge, came to an end at the Mississippi River. On my left was the I-10 Bridge over the river, which was not an option because it is illegal to run on the interstate, with a few exceptions, like when I pleaded in Arizona. That left the Huey Long Bridge on my right. It is about a mile long and an old, pedestrian-unfriendly means of travel. I decided to call Sheryl to drive me over the bridge into West Baton Rouge. I figured I would make up the mile the next day, which I did.

Port Barre, Louisiana—In Port Barre I stopped at a biker bar to get a drink.

They were preparing free meals for customers without jobs. Fare for the evening was meatloaf stew. Decided to pass on going back with Sheryl for dinner. Needless to say, I was a bit uncomfortable wearing my running clothes in the midst of leather clad, very heavily-bearded bikers. I felt like a mouse trying to be invisible in a snake pit.

Krotz Springs, Louisiana—Krotz Springs had one of the strangest sounding names of the 272 communities I ran through. I crossed a very high bridge and came down to the bottom and saw the welcome sign for Krotz Springs. I remember thinking how many times must the residents of this town have to repeat and then spell Krotz Springs. Not to mention the jokes.

DeQuincy, Louisiana—What struck me about this small town were the beautiful murals on the sides of the downtown buildings. DeQuincy was a major railroad depot in Louisiana, and is proud of its railroad museum.

Sour Lake, Texas—Sour Lake is the birthplace of Texaco Oil, which was founded in 1903.

BRIAN COLLINS, REGIONAL MANAGER AT THE DRURY INN, ASKED AHEAD IF HE COULD RUN WITH ME TO CUT AND SHOOT, TEXAS.

Cut and Shoot, Texas—Cut and Shoot had the most unusual name of any town we passed through. The regional manager of the Drury Inns, Brian, emailed me and requested to run with me one day. He was very helpful and very generous with huge discounts whenever we were in a city that had a Drury Inn. There are quite a few marathoners in the executive offices at the Drury Inn, so when Brian heard about my run, he contacted me. We ended our 20-mile run at the Cut and Shoot fire station. Brian was one of only three people I ran with during the entire run.

Brenham, Texas—Brenham is the home of Blue Bell Ice Cream. Sheryl took the plant tour while I was running and couldn't stop raving about the creamery. Brenham is also the home of Blinn College. As I ran past Blinn, I had a scowl on my face thinking about Cam Newton, the Auburn quarterback who went to Blinn before playing at Auburn. Enough said.

Giddings, Texas—Giddings marked 1,000 miles. We celebrated with a steak dinner at the Giddings Downtown Restaurant. It was a memorable evening. We celebrated the 1000 miles run and didn't mention the 1350 miles to go.

Austin, Texas—We saw the University of Texas in Austin, watched a Texas-Oklahoma baseball game, experienced the Driscoll Hotel, and spent a wonderful evening on the city's historic 6th Street. The state capitol building was magnificent.

Decatur, Texas—Decatur has a beautiful, historic town square where, as I mentioned earlier, you can find the best Texas rib eye steak and baked potato at Sweetie Pie's Ribeyes. It was like going back in time, as I imagined an old western restaurant, for the finest steak and baked potato. Baked in rosin, it is the fluffiest baked potato in the world.

MONUMENT IN TOWN CENTER IN RILEY, TEXAS. DO NOT MESS WITH TEXAS!

Riley, Texas—Running through the small hamlet of Riley, I noticed the town square had a very large plaque displaying the Ten Commandments. I'm not a lawyer, but...I was definitely in the heart of the Texas Bible belt.

Tahoka, Texas—Tahoka was the location of my first encounter with a very bad dust storm. I couldn't see much for most of the run that day. Squinting was my only defense from the blowing dust. I bought sunglasses that afternoon and wore them every day until the end of the run. If I had planned a little better, I would have realized that there is a reason why most bikers and Transamerica runners run west to east. It's the wind, stupid! I experienced only one big dust storm on this run, but the strong winds in west Texas and New Mexico were an almost daily battle.

Texico, New Mexico—Texico was the first New Mexico town I ran through just as I crossed over the Texas border. This was the beginning of my experience with the daily high winds New Mexico is noted for. My nephew's fiancée, Vanessa, who is from Albuquerque, had warned me about the strong winds. I should have taken her more seriously.

Clovis, New Mexico—Clovis is the home of Leal's Mexican Restaurant. Leal's has the finest fajitas Sheryl and I have ever had.

MOST ISOLATED RUNS WERE IN NEW MEXICO.

Taiban, New Mexico—Population: seven, Taiban had one of only two Postmasters—and a very nice one, at that—whom I spoke with on my trip.

Yeso, New Mexico—Population: six, Yeso had the other Postmaster—also very nice—I spoke with. The women Postmasters at both Taiban and Yeso said it is only a matter of time before their offices will be closed. They're just waiting.

Ft. Sumner, New Mexico—Ft. Sumner is famous as the place where Billy the Kid was killed and buried. It has a great museum and a terrific drive-in called Dairyland. Other than that, Sheryl and I were left to explore every part of the town, over and over again, for four days as we used Ft. Sumner as our base.

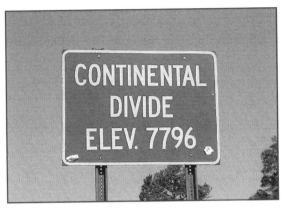

I WONDERED WHY IT SEEMED HARDER TO BREATHE WEST OF I-25 IN NEW MEXICO. CONTINENTAL DIVIDE.

Santa Rosa, New Mexico—Although I didn't actually run through Santa Rosa, we stayed there as we escaped the boredom of Ft. Sumner as I was running to the south. This was my first taste of a section of Historic Route 66. Santa Rosa is the home of a very large classic antique auto collection, part of the Route 66 attraction. We went from a Super 8 Motel in Ft. Sumner to a very nice Holiday Inn Express at a great rate in Santa Rosa. What a nice change for us.

Moriarty, New Mexico—Moriarty, was another town I didn't actually run through, but where we stayed in order for me to run farther south where there were no accommodations. It was my first smell and taste of the smoke being blown in from the Wallow fire in southeast Arizona. The smoke was so bad, I had to sleep and run with a surgical mask on. We watched the collapse of Congressman Weiner on TV as I lay in bed breathing through a mask, trying to fall asleep.

Socorro, New Mexico—Socorro is the home of New Mexico Institute of Mining and Technology, where the VLA operations center is housed. This university is also where first responders against terrorist attacks are trained. Moreover it boasts great wood fire pizza and fantastic hamburgers at the Socorro Springs Restaurant. This is where we watched the Bruins win the Stanley Cup.

THAT'S RIGHT—PIE TOWN.
THAT'S RIGHT—THE BEST!

Pie Town, New Mexico—Pie Town is the small town nearest the sign noting the Continental Divide on Route 60. There is a reason that Pie Town is named Pie Town. It is the home of the best cherry pie I've ever had. Any pie you want you'll find in Pie Town. And, yes, they have an annual pie festival that includes a pie eating contest. Also, it's one of the only spots in the U.S. from which you can see the Milky Way.

Magdalena, New Mexico—Between Magdalena and Datil, I ran past the VLA (Very

Large Array), the magnificent technological wonder that spreads over the plains of San Agustin. While running, I got to view all 27 radio antennas configured in the shape of a 'Y.' The leg of the Y crossed over Route 60, the road I was on heading toward Arizona. Magdalena is the home of the Bear Mountain Coffee House. The owner, Danielle is as nice as can be, and Bear Mountain has the best tuna on wheat in all of New Mexico.

AS I WAS FEELING GOOD, HEADED TOWARD THE VLA, I SAW THIS EYE-OPENING SIGN.

Eager-Springerville, Arizona— Eagar-Springerville was the only town in which we stayed in a non-branded motel. The Rode Inn was occupied by mostly firefighters who were there to fight and contain the Wallow Fire originating in the Southeast corner of Arizona. We got daily updates on the direction of the fire. The hotel provided guests with heavy duty surgical masks to help with the smoke. The town had been forced to evacuate the week before we arrived. Although Eager and Springerville are separate towns, they have grown together geographically.

Show Low, Arizona—Show Low got its name from a card game that determined the owner of the town when it was first established. It's a neat mountain resort town where people from the valley (Phoenix area) have second homes to escape the sweltering summer heat of the desert. The small movie theatre was a trip back in time. We saw the movie "Bad Teacher" there for $3.50.

Phoenix and Scottsdale, Arizona—I ran through Phoenix, but we stayed in Scottsdale, to the northeast. Surface streets through the area made the 114+ temperatures a little easier and safer. There was no shortage of convenience stores to stop in for a quick cold drink and Fig Newtons as I ran. What a beautiful city. This was where I noticed that the temperatures peaked later in the day, between 3:00 p.m. and 5:00 p.m., not that there is a whole lot of difference between running in 110 degrees and 114 degrees.

Litchfield Park, Arizona—Home of the Wigwam Resort, Litchfield Park was the nicest and most comfortable place we stayed on the entire trip. Daily swims in the huge pools provided a great deal of relief and were very relaxing and therapeutic for my muscles. (More later.) We needed a place like this because running the last 100 miles in Arizona was very tough.

Tonopah, Arizona—Tonopah was the start of the only stretch I had to run on the interstate, I-10. The Tonopah exit had just a couple of gas stations and a truck stop, and it marked the end of one of my worst running days. It was here that I decided it was time to get a Camelbak, an insulated lightweight backpack that carries sixty-four ounces of fluid. It has a long plastic tube coming out of the reservoir to make it easy to drink from.

WELCOME TO BLYTHE, CALIFORNIA, JUST OVER THE ARIZONA BORDER.

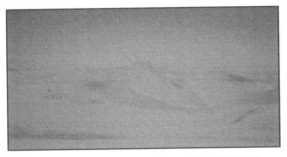

THE IMPERIAL SAND DUNES NEAR EL CENTRO, CALIFORNIA. A BEAUTIFUL AREA OF SAND DUNES WITH 114 DEGREES AND A WIND LIKE STANDING IN FRONT OF A JET ENGINE.

Blythe, California—Blythe was the first city past the California border. It was here that I started getting excited realizing I was actually going to finish my run across the country. It was also our home base for a few days as I ran through the farm lands of southeast California. Blythe had a great diner, The Courtesy Coffee Shop.

Glamis, California—Glamis is the home of the Imperial Sand Dunes where dune buggy enthusiasts from all over the world come to cruise the dunes. The scenery is beautiful, but the heat is like a furnace. It marked my final run before we headed to El Centro, just a few miles from the Mexican border. Despite Sheryl's concerns about being so close to Mexico, we had no problems and the people were extremely nice. We stayed about three miles from the border. We saw our first In-N-Out Burger restaurant near our hotel. I was dying for a burger, but I promised Julie I would wait so she could buy us her favorite hamburger.

THE SMALL TOWN OF JULIAN IN THE MOUNTAINS EAST OF SAN DIEGO HAS GREAT PIE AND BEAUTIFUL SCENERY.

Julian, California—Julian is a quaint tourist town with plenty of pies and a very steep, windy road leading up the mountain to the town. I didn't spend much time in Julian since I was scared to death of the height and the poor running conditions leading to and from the town. The walk/run up the mountain was a killer, with a scary, steep incline. Although the view was beautiful, I was glad to leave quickly.

Poway, California—Poway is a nice suburban town at the foot of the mountains, just before entering the metro San Diego area. It had nice wide sidewalks to run the final few miles into San Diego. Running past the Miramar Marine Corps Air Base on my final 20-mile run was neat. I heard jet planes overhead and had a chance to remember my journey across the country as I inched my way to Crystal Pier at Pacific Beach, where I would get to hug my daughter and step into the ocean, exactly as I had dreamed of doing.

My dream had come true. Very cool!

A Special Appreciation: The Jewish Connection

Among the many benefits of being Jewish, the most significant is what I refer to as "The Jewish Connection." This seems to be a universal phenomenon, experienced not just by Sheryl and me, but by virtually every Jew. No matter where you are in the world, if you meet another Jew, the longer you talk, the more you realize that there is a link to mutual friends or family.

If, on the rare occasion I met another Jew and there were no links, there is still the comfort and connection of being with another Jew in another place in the world. Maybe it's because there are so few of us.

With the help of Nefesh B'Nefesh, the Jewish organization that helps Jews in North America become Israeli citizens, arrangements were made along our route for Sheryl and me to attend services. Since my mother and father had passed away recently, just months apart, I wanted to attend services to remember them both.

We were fortunate to have visited seven synagogues along our route and I want to recognize each one for its members' kindness and friendship to Sheryl and me. Those Friday evenings allowed me to escape the running world of the unknown and retreat to a familiar place I never really appreciated as a child, but which gave me comfort as a runner with an unknown future. I did not pray; I just felt at peace in familiar and friendly surroundings.

Mobile, Alabama—Ahavas Chesed Synagogue. We were fortunate to be at this beautiful synagogue on a Friday night when a Jewish a cappella group from New York performed. It was a beautiful performance and we were invited by the Rabbi to join the congregation for a full dinner. As I was being introduced to members of the congregation, I recognized a fraternity brother of mine, Larry, whom I had not seen in over 42 years.

New Orleans, Louisiana—Beth Shalom Synagogue. Actually, it is located in Metairie. I was asked to speak to the congregation about my run across the country. When hurricane Katrina had hit New Orleans, members of this synagogue had to rescue the Torah from the ark by rowboat to get it to a safe place. The congregation was extremely friendly and we had a great experience.

Baton Rouge, Louisiana—Beth Shalom Synagogue. After the Friday night service, Sheryl and I were enjoying dessert and meeting some of the members. A woman came up to me and said that she had known a Bea and Victor Cohen from Montgomery, Alabama. I had mentioned my parents name during the service when the rabbi asks the congregation if anyone was saying "Kaddish," the prayer for family members who have passed away during the year. I raised my hand and mentioned my parents' names.

I was shocked and taken aback by this woman, Rhea, who was someone I had grown up with but had not seen in over forty-six years. Her husband, Raymond, a professor at LSU, had also gone to the University of Alabama but was a few years ahead of me. We had a two-hour breakfast together the next morning, and Sheryl and I got a royal tour of the LSU campus. Old acquaintances in a chance meeting after forty-six years—truly amazing and enjoyable!

Lake Charles, Louisiana—Temple Sinai. We stayed in Lake Charles for a few days because the areas I was running through just north had no motels. This was one of those areas where Sheryl had to drive hundreds of miles a day so I could run my 20 miles. Temple Sinai was an older, beautiful, historic temple, but was in the throes of a slow death. Few Jewish families remained in Lake Charles, traditionally ranked as one of the least desirable cities in the country, according to what I had read about long before my first visit to the city back in 1977. I was there on business and staying in a Days Inn when I heard the news that Elvis had died. I was not a big Elvis fan, but it's one of those "I'll never forget where I was when…" moments. That, coupled with its low desire ranking makes it memorable.

Other than a very enjoyable service, what I remembered most was that the woman sitting across from us in the sanctuary was a police officer, in uniform. I had assumed she was security, but she was a member. Another first. As I left the Temple, I looked back and knew that it would cease to exist in a few years. The fifteen members attending walked to their cars and drove away. Although I'd been there only an hour, the thought of its demise really bothered me. Another part of the Jewish community disappearing.

Houston, Texas—Congregation Beth Yeshurun. Timing is everything. Not only were we able to stay in the Houston area for ten days while I ran to the north, we were there over Passover. Thankfully, we were in a big city to be able to celebrate Passover with, if not our own families, at least with other Jewish families. Plus, it was a nice break for Sheryl to see some other shops besides Walmart and Dollar General. Fortunately, Nefesh B'Nefesh had made arrangements for us to spend the first night of Passover with Cantor David Propis and his family and invited friends, and with Rabbi David Rosen and his family the second night.

We had no idea that this was the largest conservative synagogue in the United States, with over 2500 member families. This synagogue has five rabbis, three sanctuaries, and a museum. It sits on a very large campus where the parking lot was so big, and we had to park so far away that a gentleman in a golf cart gave us a lift to the entrance.

We went to what we thought was the main sanctuary because it was so big, but realized afterwards we were in a smaller, more traditional service. The main service was in the main sanctuary, so we thought. When we finally connected with Rabbi Rosen (he recognized me from the red running shoes I was wearing because my dress shoes wouldn't fit. My feet had grown two shoe sizes), he informed us that we needed to go down the hall to see the "REAL" main sanctuary—the largest and one of the most beautiful I have ever seen.

On this Friday night with nothing special happening in the way of holidays or special services, the attendance was over 700—as we later learned, a usual Friday night attendance, unheard of in virtually any other Jewish place of worship.

The Passover services were very enjoyable on both nights. The congregants could not have been more welcoming to Sheryl and me, and we were later invited to Steve Rudoff's house for a wonderful barbeque. A new acquaintance that night, Gordon, made arrangements with his son, the student manager of the University of Texas baseball team, to have us as his guests for the UT-Oklahoma baseball game in Austin.

The members of this congregation were so friendly and warm to us that we seriously considered moving to Houston once I finished the run. The only thing lacking in Houston was proximity to the water, thus our selection of Tampa.

Sheryl and I will never forget our ten-day stay in Houston over Passover and our visit on the return trip back east.

A very special thank you to Rabbi David Rosen and his family, Cantor David Propis and his family, and to Steve Rudoff and his family.

Austin, Texas—Agudas Achim. The Friday our car broke down in Austin, arrangements had been made by Nefesh B'Nefesh for us to attend services at Agudas Achim Synogogue. Fortunately our car problem was resolved in time for us to make it to the services. A small group of people, about 25, attended Shabbat services in their smaller chapel. The services were led by a male and a female rabbi. It was unique in that there was discussion between the rabbis and the congregants throughout the service.

Unbeknownst to Sheryl and me, we were in Austin around the University of Texas spring graduation period. Sitting in services were family members of the graduate students who had just defended their doctoral dissertations and were days away from graduation. As we were being greeted by members after the service, we were invited to a Shabbat dinner by a family that had just flown in from California to see their daughter receive her Ph.D.

We had a very enjoyable dinner with the family and two other students, one, a former Israeli soldier, also receiving her Ph.D.

Albuquerque, New Mexico—Congregation Albert. While staying just south of Albuquerque, in Belen, we met my nephew's future in-laws, Jeff and Julia, and attended Friday night services with them at their synagogue in Albuquerque. The service was packed because that night the new officers of the congregation were being installed. It was a very large, beautiful synagogue, and the members were very welcoming to us. Afterwards we had dinner and got a taste of student life near the University of New Mexico campus.

These seven visits along the running path provided Sheryl and me a brief connection to a familiar environment and a mental safe haven from the huge unknown that was our future. For the hour or so that we spent in the safe and familiar and friendly surroundings of a Jewish world, we felt at home away from home, and it felt good.

CHAPTER **16** SIXTEEN

Why?

....

Losing our home and business gave me pause. I asked myself a pretty basic question. "Why and what am I here for?"

I thought it was quite apropos in my situation to ask the most appropriate question anyone could ask himself. The answer is really one's mission statement. *Where do I go from here? What have I missed? What do I want to do? If I was lying on my death bed reflecting back on my life, what is it that I can do now, that would erase regret and put a smile on my face?*

I had my answer a week after we closed our store. It was actually very simple. My purpose in life was to get the most out of my life by experiencing as much of what this world has to offer.

I sat back and asked myself if I had been able to take advantage of what the world had to offer with respect to sights, sounds, experiences, places and, most importantly, simply feeling good. I also evaluated my relationships with others I knew and with strangers.

I came to the realization that I had only scratched the surface of all aspects of my mission statement. But there was a quick solution—just run across the country. See, experience, feel, and meet; all in one travel kit. I would see places and things I've never experienced. I'd feel great, both physically and mentally. And I'd get to meet people I'd never meet otherwise.

Everything wrapped up in 2350 miles. A very nice package.

Of course, I didn't really think of all of this before we set out on the run, but it did turn out to cover all the bases and at least partially fulfill my dream. We saw big chunks of eight states as I ran over U.S., state, and county roads. We saw beautiful scenery, beautiful towns (large and small), natural beauty, man-made beauty, and we met some of the most incredible people—ordinary men and women who are the salt of the earth. We got to taste regional foods in each state, and that was amazing. I was exceptionally fortunate in that regard because I had to eat so much each day.

After we closed the store, I feverishly went on the computer to job search. I had to get an income and quick. After a week or so, realizing that I was a dinosaur in the modern world of technology, I began to question what I was doing. Why am I—out of habit and not really thinking this through—just trying to continue on the same path as the past 37 years? I really needed to take a step back and figure out what I *wanted* to do—not what I felt I *had* to do.

That's when it dawned on me that I could break from the norm and drag out this mothball dream of mine; running across the country. It took all of five minutes to make the decision.

In my head, I was out the door and headed to Jacksonville Beach, with the details to be worked out later. Once we were on our way after the very brief planning stage, I wondered why it took hitting rock bottom to get this life dream up and rolling. I was excited, and the sense of freedom was overwhelming. We actually had to get used to having so much freedom and very little responsibility. I felt like I was back at my high school graduation and feeling so good and free with an extended five-and-a-half month summer vacation ahead of me and not a care in the world.

The trip down to Jacksonville from Atlanta was filled with anticipation of what lay ahead for Sheryl and me. The duties were simple—I'd run 20 miles a day and Sheryl would do everything else. We learned after a few weeks that the division of duties was lopsided. I was having the time of my life, minus some physical adjustments such as blisters, raw nipples, and toenails turning black. Sheryl had the hard part of finding hotels, getting food, washing clothes, and filling five hours a day with entertaining herself. It all evened out after some simple adjustments.

MY DAILY DROP-OFF SOMEWHERE IN NEW MEXICO. ANOTHER WONDERFUL DAY OF PEACE, QUIET, AND NO TECHNOLOGY.

For the first time in my adult life—after 37 years of it—I was a free man. No responsibilities of a business: employees, finances, liability, insurance, attorneys, accountants, cash flow, inventory, computers, customers, vendors, advertising schedules, merchandising. Just my wife and me and at age 60, out on a cross-country run. Plus, I was fulfilling a dream and beginning my mission to get more out of my life.

It's not that we were suffering before this all happened. We actually loved what we did. We were fortunate to be a part of parents' (our customers') lives as they experienced one of the biggest joys of life—having a baby, usually the first.

We took our responsibility very seriously, though it wasn't just business. We wanted our customers to have the nursery of their dreams, and we felt that we needed to help each couple have the best experience possible. Most of the expectant women we served had their dream nursery envisioned since they played with dolls as children. We had fun and thoroughly enjoyed being a part of their event. Sheryl was incredible with customers and had developed a wonderful reputation.

When was the last time you sat back—alone—and questioned what you were really doing and how content you were? I never had in all those years. Considering I had to work for a living and had a wife and three children to support, I was pretty happy and content with my businesses and what they afforded my family. With never a moment's reflection or thought of alternatives, I just kept plugging away, day after day, year after year, just like most folks.

Yet it seems reasonable to question your existence and quality of life at least once a year, whether you can actually do anything to change it or not. It's the questioning of yourself that may just open some doors of opportunity that could lead to something more gratifying. My "quality of life" check did just that.

We got so wrapped up in our more immediate needs that we overlooked what was really important to us. Was my destiny as a human being to work and have an occasional respite to fulfill my personal needs? And don't those needs usually wind up being the needs of others, such as your family members?

Look at it in relation to time; each of us is in this world but a nano second. The planet, from a scientist's point-of-view, is about four and a half billion years old. From a biblical perspective, it's about 6,000 years old. Whichever measurement you embrace, a life of around 80 years is a very short time.

Why not enjoy that brief period as much as possible? You only have one trip through life. Since most of us are Average Joes, we can pretty much figure the impact we have in our lifetime will be small, relative to the grand scheme of life in the universe. The next time you take off in a plane, look out the window and see how small and insignificant people and things really are from the perspective of cruising altitude.

Unless you are a Winston Churchill, John Kennedy, Gandhi, or Mother Teresa, your impact will be felt only by those closest to you—in relationships and geographically. After death, as time passes, your life and how you lived will become a fading memory. Those closest to you will remember longer and with more intensity. Those who have minimal contact with you will forget you more quickly. This is even more reason to live a full life, even more reason to have a dream and live that dream. Do it for yourself; others really don't care. They have their own lives to construct and live. Try not to be naïve and think that your life and what you do with it is on others' minds. Your life and how you choose to live it should be of your choosing, not made to fit someone else's standards.

There are those in the world who hold important positions that have dramatic impact on others. But even those people with such a strong sense of duty, morality, obligation, honor, responsibility, and the need to help others must take a step back and ask, "But what about me?" I'm sure each one has looked into the mirror and begged for anonymity if only for a day. There is a need, at some point, to protect your own self.

My behavior directly affects my family and friends. It also affects those in my immediate vicinity: neighbors and anyone with whom I come in close contact regularly. Other than that, I am a very small part of this world. My importance is miniscule. There is no need to feel bad when you realize this. That's just the way it is from a practical standpoint. It's also a very liberating thought.

Here's the paradox. We may be very unimportant in relationship to the universe, but we are very important to ourselves and those closest to us. Treat yourself as though you are worthy of a full, fun, and more meaningful life without concern for others' opinions or critical eyes. You are free to set your own course, regardless of what the norms may dictate.

What a refreshing way to look at life! I realize my lack of importance in the world. This realization removes the pressure to perform or reach for the stars or otherwise feel the need to compete or meet others' expectations. It allows for personal dreams and goals to be pursued without the unrealistic notion that others really care.

Some people are destined for fame and have a dramatic impact on others—presidents, writers, superstars, actors, the people on the front of newspapers and magazines and in front of television cameras—those whom others look up to for a variety of reasons—good and bad. These people, intentionally or unintentionally, have placed themselves in a position of influence by which they can have dramatic impact on others' lives.

They are the ones with the stressful burden that they must carry because so many people are counting on them for guidance and inspiration. They may have fame and fortune, but chances are they rarely have time to look after themselves and their own contentment. It may be rare to find a famous person who is genuinely happy. Fame has its price, and it's usually a high one. Often famous or influential people begin to believe the headlines, and their lives are guided by a thirst to please and be noticed. They lose their personal mission statement for contentment.

For the rest of us, there is the luxury of virtual anonymity. I told my kids years ago that my goal in life is total anonymity. I want to be able to wander the earth invisibly. I am fully capable of dipping into social settings and conducting myself in an appropriate manner, but mostly I want to go through life taking in as much as possible of what this world has to offer. That's what makes me feel alive, gratified, and content.

My run across the country was my opportunity to be the earth traveler I always dreamed of being—literally. One day I looked around at the vast nothingness I was running through and felt that I was a combination of Paul Bunyan, Johnny Appleseed, and the Kung Fu character played by David Carradine. I was travelling the back roads of the country, experiencing what our country offered me. There were no expectations and no timetable, except my own. I had never felt freer and more content with my life than those days of solitude with nothing but the abundance of nature as company.

I don't profess to think that I have found the universal answer to contentment for everyone. I have found mine and that is all that matters. Anyone who gives himself or herself the opportunity can dream of the ideal existence and strive to immerse oneself in that. Most won't stop long enough to break away from the daily cycle they are in to even contemplate the notion. Eighty years is only a blink of an eye. Each one of us deserves to get the most out of that nano second of time in this life.

People seem to be missing the point when it comes to improving their quality of life and experiencing the joy of traveling through that life. Most look for pleasure outside themselves. They believe material things, that special relationship, that dream job, or acceptance from peers will fulfill them.

All of this is fine if it is kept in perspective. What about yourself, your thoughts, your contentment, your sense of fulfillment? Not just those from accomplishments, but from realizing your dreams and developing the ability to simply feel good.

We are taught to feel guilty if we're not engaged in productive activity. We believe it is wrong to "waste" time. Were you put on this earth to be nothing but a "producer," someone who must always be accomplishing? You can ease up; take time to just relax by doing nothing.

COMING DOWN OUT OF THE MOUNTAINS IN NEW MEXICO.

Somewhere along the line you began to believe you had to produce, to create, to accomplish. Try unlearning the compulsion to produce, and just sit in a park and feel the sun on your face; smell the fresh air. You are, in fact, accomplishing something. You're allowing yourself to feel content and relaxed for a change. Your mind needs it and so does your body.

If you go on a trip, don't you want to experience what is offered? Don't you visit the points of interest, explore the different areas, eat the local food and take in the local color? Why should life be any different? You are, in fact, on a trip. You start your journey of life at birth, and when you die your journey ends. Why not fill the years in between with as much adventure, as much fulfillment, and as much contentment as possible? Is your journey simply a series of years filled with doing the same thing, day after day, year after year until, before you know it, the months have become years and the years, decades? Life is not about only work and engaging others.

I saw my run across the country as a brief yet complete trip through a portion of my life. As I progressed through each state, I took in more and more and learned to appreciate each day for what it brought me: sights, smells, sounds, sensations, and contact with others I hadn't met before. Each day was a singular adventure.

I rarely looked at my watch because time didn't matter. My pace was so consistent that I could sense the amount of time I had been running. The further into the run, the more I just experienced and enjoyed, and felt free and good.

After I passed through the town of Mountainair, New Mexico, my path entered a vista of desert with beautiful mountains in the distance. I was wearing a surgical mask because of the smoke in the air from the forest fires blowing toward me from Arizona. Despite being able to see the air I was breathing—which really sucked (no pun intended)—the view was magnificent. It made me appreciate the tremendous opportunity I was afforded by losing everything and then taking the occasion to take a step back, readjust my focus, and fulfill my dream.

Each day, I looked forward to my run and enjoyment of the day; being in the moment. A lot of people asked me during and after my run how I was able to motivate myself each day to go out and run 20 miles. It was obvious to me that they were looking at the physical aspect of the run and not the esoteric opportunities it presented. I saw it as a gift that I was not going to squander.

CHAPTER **17** SEVENTEEN

Singing in the Rain— Porn Shop Stop

One day of rain; that's all I had. It may sound like good luck, but for someone who loves running in the rain, and who was exposed to very high temperatures most days, it was disappointing. There is nothing like a nice run in a warm summer shower.

On my one day's run in the rain, I started out running with my good friend Alan, who was riding his bike alongside me toward Ft. Walton Beach, Florida. After about eight miles, Alan turned around in anticipation of the expected storm. I continued, looking forward to a run in the rain. Having spent fourteen years in Boston, I have always taken weather reports with a grain of salt. Weather conditions were rarely as good—or as bad—as predicted. They say in Boston, "If you don't like the weather, just wait a few minutes; it will change."

The clouds were really getting very dark and the temperature had dropped a little. When the rain started, it wasn't what I had been looking forward to; it was a hard, driving rain and colder than I liked.

These weren't the worst conditions I had experienced, though. Training for the Boston marathon in the winter of '95-'96 had, by far, the most uncomfortable conditions I've ever run in, thus my intense dislike for running in cold weather.

The rain turned into a storm, which included a driving wind. I was okay until I remembered I had my cell phone. I hadn't thought of putting it in anything to protect it. That became my biggest concern at the moment. By mile 18, cars were sliding on the pavement, it was becoming hard to see, and it was cold. I decided, for the first time on the run, to stop where I could and have Sheryl pick me up. I had a very long trip ahead of me so I wasn't going to take chances.

Ahead of me I saw a small house with strings of lights all over it. I knew it was a business but couldn't make out the sign. I walked up to the front door and went inside. I was soaking wet and I asked the man at the front desk if I could stand on the front mat and call my wife. He nodded and I called Sheryl. As I waited for her to answer, I looked around and realized I was in a porn shop. Sheryl answered and I tried to give her directions to the place. I gave her the best directions I could, considering I could hardly see as I approached the store. In a very low voice, I told her to just look for the porn shop with blinking lights.

When I noticed that I had dripped water all over the floor, I apologized to the man who glanced at me and nodded once more. After a few calls back and forth with Sheryl about the location, she finally pulled up. I asked the man if I could grab a plastic bag from the garbage can to protect my phone as I ran out to the car. He nodded again—a man of few words. I ran to the car and we drove away. I was soaking wet but all I cared about was not damaging my phone. From that point on, I carried my phone in a small baggie, which served to protect it from my sweat since it never rained again. This was my only link to the world for most of the trip.

Sanctuary from the storm, in a porn shop called "Special Moments." As good a place as any, I suppose.

A Random Act of Kindness

On day sixty-seven of the run, May 25, I was running in the hot Texas sun. I had my water belt with two 10-ounce bottles of water attached. I tried to ration my water over the twenty miles so that I'd have some left when I completed my run for the day. My concerns were that our car would break down before Sheryl could pick me up or Sheryl would get lost (a 40 percent chance every day), so I gave myself a little margin for error in case I was stuck waiting. Unfortunately, the water bottles weren't insulated and the water would rapidly reach air temperature—hot! It did the job of keeping me hydrated, but hot water was hard to swallow.

I was running alongside the road when a gentleman in a truck pulled up beside me and asked if I was okay. I thanked him and told him I was just out for a run. Before he pulled away I asked him if he had any water. He rummaged through his ice chest and I saw he had a six-pack of beer and a bottle one quarter full of Gatorade, which he offered to me. I gratefully accepted it. As he pulled away, I waved and thanked him again. He had offered a refreshing, cold drink just when I needed it.

I continued my run. Later on, the same truck came toward me and pulled off the road and onto the grass. A hand extended from the front window—holding a large bottle of Gatorade. The same guy who had asked me if I was okay earlier said, "I thought you could use some more." I just stood there stunned.

This man had driven to the next town, conducted his business, gone to a store and returned with this bottle of cold Gatorade for me. I shook his hand and thanked him and watched in wonder as he drove away.

A total stranger, someone who had no reason to help me, went to the effort and expense of returning and bringing me a drink. I was so overwhelmed by this rare act of kindness that I just stood there. The fact that he gave a little extra to a fellow human being made me feel like a million bucks. I continued my run and began to think about the saying "one good turn deserves another."

One of the many experiences I got out of this run across the country was that I found myself returning to basic courtesies; the things that are the simplest, yet most important and meaningful in life. Even before the good Gatorade deed in Texas, I found myself going out of my way to help other people, even animals.

When I was passing through Ft. Walton Beach, Florida, I knew I was headed into that thunderstorm. As I ran through a small residential area, I saw an elderly woman in her housecoat trying to make her way up her gravel driveway with her walker, trying to bring her three recycling bins back into her garage before the rains came. She was barely making progress, trying to maneuver her walker while carrying one bin. The gravel made it very difficult for her.

I picked up the two remaining bins and carried them up the driveway to the garage. She thanked me and I was on my way. For a brief moment in time, a stranger stopped what he was doing to lend a hand to another. I helped her. That small act of kindness made me feel good (probably like the Gatorade trucker later on in Texas). The woman reminded me of my mom. She, too, was probably someone's mother.

Courtesies seem rarer in our modern times. I got back to the simple things on my run, and it felt good—really good.

CHAPTER  NINETEEN

The Cancer Biker

Two days before I crossed into New Mexico, I was stopped by a Texas state trooper who asked if I was okay and told me that a man had called the station to report seeing a man running on the highway for two days in a row. He thought they should check on it.

The trooper told me that this man rides his motorcycle from Plains, Texas, to Lubbock, every Monday through Friday in three-week increments. He makes the trip, which takes an hour and a half each way, to the hospital for chemotherapy to treat his prostate cancer.

I thanked the officer for checking on me and I finished my run that day about 20 miles from the New Mexico border.

The next day, running towards Plains, Texas, the last town before crossing into New Mexico, I saw a three-wheeled Harley approaching. It veered onto the shoulder. The driver, a man who appeared to be in his late 60s or early 70s, took his helmet off. He was big, about six-foot-two. He told me that he had seen me before and asked what I was doing out here on the road.

I explained what I was doing and asked him where he was going. He told me that he rides his bike from Plains to Lubbock for his chemo sessions. He said, "Can you believe I drive three hours round-trip for 15 minutes of chemo?" He looked down at the ground and just shook his head. I asked how he was doing, and he said, "So far, so good." We talked for a few minutes more. I shook his hand, thanked him for his concern for my safety, and wished him good health. He rode away.

Later, down the road, I became very thirsty. It was a rough day; the closer I got to New Mexico, the stronger the winds blew. I was battling the headwinds all day, not to mention the 100-plus degree temperature. Even on a flat road, the winds were tough to run against. For the first time, my lips were cracking from the heat and dryness.

I was beginning to feel the effects of thirst and the wind, when I saw a work crew about thirty yards off the road. As I approached, I saw two Hispanic men with a huge wrench, working on some pipes. As I approached them, I saw a beautiful sight: a bright orange, round Igloo water cooler.

I didn't want to startle them so I knocked on their truck. When they turned around, I asked if they had some extra water. They just looked at me, which made me realize they didn't speak English. In my very poor tenth grade Spanish I said, "Agua?"

They looked at each other and smiled. I didn't care what they thought of my pathetic attempt at Spanish; I just wanted some water. One of them pointed to the Igloo and I nodded. I knew better than to look around for one of those cone-shaped paper cups. Road crews don't use cups, something I'd discovered in Louisiana when I stopped to ask a crew for some water. That time I looked around and asked the guys where the cups were. They looked at me like I was the biggest wimp in the world. The succinct reply was, "No cups."

I cupped my hand under the small spigot and drank the ice cold water. If you've never been in a similar situation, you can't imagine how good that water tasted. There was as much water as I needed; ice cold water going down a dusty, parched throat. My cracked lips felt better from running my tongue over them with the water in my mouth.

I hadn't yet perfected the art of drinking from my hands so, as usual, my sleeves were soaking wet. Even that felt good. I took a few more gulps and thanked the men, "Muchas gracias." They motioned for me to take more. I took a few more sips, shook their hands, walked back to the road, and waved to them.

I felt great except for the driving wind in my face that seemed to have gotten even stronger. About half an hour later, I heard a truck slowing behind me and turned to see the two guys who had given me water. They were waving at me to come get more water. I crossed the road, and drank some more of that magical ice-cold water. Sleeves wet again, I thanked them and watched as they drove off. Those guys were making sure I didn't get dehydrated on their watch.

About an hour later, a truck pulled onto the shoulder and approached me. It was my two new friends again. They pointed to the Igloo and I gladly drank their water for a third time. This time, as I shook their hands, I felt the need to pull out my Spanish and again said, "Muchas gracias." Again, they looked at each other and snickered. I can only imagine what they said about my attempt at Spanish as they drove away.

These two guys decided to do what they could to make my exposure to the elements a little bit easier. They had no idea what my purpose was. It was another encounter with nice people. They wanted nothing in return except to see that I had enough water. They didn't have to stop for me at all, let alone twice. They could have honked and waved as they passed those two times but, instead, they took a few moments to go out of their way and extend some kindness. In French, it's called "lagniappe"—a little extra.

As I approached the very small town of Plains, Texas, I stopped in front of a small garage and waited for Sheryl to pick me up. I noticed a familiar three-wheeled motorcycle. Inside the garage were three older men. One was approaching me.

It was the man who had asked the trooper to check on me and later stopped on his way to his chemo treatment. He introduced me to his two friends and we talked. I asked if they had computers or access to the Internet. I had decided to include this man in my blog for the day, so I wanted to see if he had Internet access. They shook their heads and my friend said that they didn't get involved with that stuff. I liked him even more.

About that time, Sheryl pulled up and got out to meet the guys. Then she and I went across the street to Dairy Queen to eat. From there, I watched as the three friends hung out together.

I watched the three older men—probably in their late 60s or early 70s—do the same thing that three teens would do; just hang out. The sight made me smile. I thought about the man and his daily trips to Lubbock for chemo. I hope he is one of the survivors. He seemed to know how to enjoy life—he and his two friends.

CHAPTER TWENTY

Reconnecting After 43 Years

What does it mean when you say that you grew up with someone? To me, it means from elementary through junior high and high school you shared the same environment and experiences. You may not have been best friends, but there is a very strong bond that develops with those with whom you have shared common childhood experiences. I reaped the pleasure and fun of that bond as Sheryl and I lingered in the Houston area for ten days.

As I began my run, I had no idea that, along the way I would hear from and meet so many people whom I had not thought of in decades. There are two people with whom I grew up in Montgomery, Alabama, whom I have stayed in contact with over the years: Alan and Mary.

Both Alan and Mary were major supporters of my run and followed me daily, for which I am eternally grateful. Nothing beats old friends.

Along the way, after 43 years, I reconnected with Dickie, (as I knew him then; Richard to his wife, current circle of friends, and business associates). I mention him because our reconnecting was one of the best things that came out of my run.

Dickie and I went to Bear Elementary School, Cloverdale Junior High School and Lanier High School together. We lost touch when we graduated from high school even though we both went to The University of Alabama. But it was the common experiences in Montgomery that brought us back together. I got to relive a part of my past with someone I last saw on our high school graduation night, all those years ago.

Dickie and I were not good friends, not even friends, actually. We knew each other; our paths crossed at school and during after-school activities, and that was about it. I knew he lived behind our elementary school, but I had never been to his house, nor he to mine. We both knew each other's friends. It was that kind of casual relationship. But the common link, along with my connection to Alan and Mary, was that we had the same history. When you're 60 years old, how many people do you have such a relationship with? Childhood friends grow up, move away and, with few exceptions, you never hear about them or from them again, except for an occasional class reunion, or through conversations with others. Now, of course, the social media offer constant communication.

While I was in Louisiana, Mary mentioned by email that Dickie lived outside of

Houston and I should stop by to see him if I was in the area. In an effort to stay away from running through a big city like Houston, I plotted a route just to the north, along Route 105. I realized that Sheryl and I would be in the Houston area for about ten days because of the size of the area and because the Passover holiday was coming up and I planned to take a few days off from running.

I wanted to celebrate the holiday and stay in a nicer hotel before we headed into the desolate parts of west Texas and through New Mexico and Arizona. I had, briefly, looked at the maps of New Mexico and Arizona and realized that the last half of my run was going to be through deserts and mountains, which left a very bad feeling in my stomach. No need to get nervous before I had to though, so I put those maps away. I'd figure it out when I actually got there.

However, I had to plot my course around Houston because we had to determine where we would be when the time came to fly to Birmingham for my niece's wedding on May 21. I never liked the idea of planning too far ahead because that put pressure on me to meet a timetable, which I didn't want to do. But in trying to determine which airport we would fly from, I had to be pretty precise. We couldn't use tickets to fly from Lubbock, Texas, if I got hurt or the car broke down and we were just west of Houston. Or, if things were going really well, I would have hated to have to slow down in order to fly out of Lubbock when I could have made it to Albuquerque, New Mexico.

WE MET UP WITH A CHILDHOOD FRIEND IN MAGNOLIA, TEXAS. WE
HADN'T SEEN EACH OTHER IN MORE THAN 40 YEARS.

So I planned my run and we made our reservations to fly out of Lubbock. As it turned out, we were right on the money. This meant spending ten days in the Houston area. This is where the miles piled up because we used Houston or, more specifically, The Woodlands just north of the city, as our home base for 120 miles of running. Each of these days we decided to drive the extra miles to drop me off each morning and pick me up after each run. This allowed us to stay at a very nice hotel at a great rate over a longer period. Brian, the regional manager of the Drury Inn located in The Woodlands, gave us a terrific rate for a suite. He happened to be a marathoner and took great interest in my run. He even ran 20 miles with me one day.

The ten days we stayed at the Drury Inn in The Woodlands more than made up for the really crappy motels we stayed in during my run through Mississippi and parts of Louisiana.

The Houston stay afforded us the opportunity to spend some time with Dickie and his wife, Ginger, who live on a 14-acre farm that includes a beautiful pond, a few cows, a horse, a house, a big garage, a swimming pool, and a small guest house. During the weeks leading up to our arrival in Houston, he and I stayed in touch via email. He was also following my daily blog.

Sheryl and I drove to Magnolia, just northwest of Houston, about 20 minutes from the hotel, to meet Dickie and Ginger at the annual Depot Fair Day in the small town center. Magnolia is a neat little town with a small downtown area and an historic train depot.

It was a typical small town spring fair with arts, crafts, food, and local talent. Dickie told me that he was a member of a blacksmith association that was putting on a demonstration that day, and to go to the mock blacksmith shop and ask for Richard when I got there. He said no one knew him as Dickie, not even his wife. It was very strange thinking of Dickie as Richard—way too formal for the Dickie I knew. I guess if I had told him my name was now Dickie, he would have thought it equally strange and awkward. It wasn't a fluid roll off the tongue like Dickie.

It was a beautiful spring day when we arrived at the fair. The best thing about small towns is the lack of traffic and the ease of parking. Sheryl and I had lived in Atlanta and Boston so, from a maneuvering standpoint, this was a true pleasure. We slowly scanned the area looking for someone I remembered only as an 18-year-old. I couldn't find Dickie, so I asked a gentleman if he could help. He pointed him out, not ten feet from me. I went up to him and put my arm around his shoulder. He turned around and we both smiled. We shook hands and hugged. Forty-three years. Not best friends, not even close friends, just two guys who had known each other since first grade.

What's the most appropriate thing for two people to say after so long? I don't know, but we just started talking about the present; family stuff, work, the run, blacksmithing, Texas, Houston, Alabama football...

As we got reacquainted, the conversation moved toward the earlier years. We spent the most time discussing Bear School: the kids and teachers. We threw names around that had not been thought of, let alone spoken by us, in decades. We smiled and laughed as names and events were drawn from our memories. I asked Dickie if he remembered the name of the Bear School janitor; he looked at me and couldn't tap that particular memory chip. When I said Luther, he stared at me in disbelief. How did I remember his name after more than 50 years? We laughed.

The names began to tumble out—Kathy, Billy, Ms. Hardaway, our principal, Johnny, Madeline, David, Twinkle, Mary, Clay, Doug, Bill, Steven, Woody, Crawford, Shelly, and on and on.

We went through Cloverdale memories and then Lanier. Then The Soul Division band surfaced. Dickie was in a very good band starting at Cloverdale, and they played at a lot of our school dances, and were a big part of our growing-up experience. They also won a number of Battle of the Bands competitions and even competed nationally. Dickie told me that Andy, a prominent cardiologist in Birmingham, had died. I was pretty upset. We're too young to die. Ironically, he had had a heart attack while driving and died in an auto accident.

For a few hours on that beautiful sunny day in Magnolia, Texas, Dickie and I were kids again. We had grown up together and had our own little world from which to pull our good memories. Sheryl and Ginger were talking about current stuff and were enjoying themselves, but not like Dickie and me. We were reliving the good old days; the days when we played on the same peewee football team, Phillip 66, at Bear School. I remembered we both played guard. We were small so why we played guard I'll never know.

Sheryl and I were able to see Dickie and Ginger again the next Saturday at another HABA (Houston Area Blacksmith Association) demonstration weekend. This time it was located outside an authentic medieval castle, complete with moat, weaponry, and feast. Not only did we have a great time with them, but we learned a lot about the craft of blacksmiths, who create products out of metal, as opposed to the craft of farriers, who shoe horses. The weather was again beautiful and we had a great time with friends.

Not only was I fulfilling my dream of running across the country, I was reliving my past with a long-lost friend. The importance of what I was doing was punctuated by the fun time I had in Magnolia, Texas, with Dickie; a very memorable time with an old friend.

CHAPTER **21** TWENTY-ONE

Texas

I had been to Dallas a few times for business, but I never really got a feel for the city or the state of Texas. Actually, I never really cared that much about getting a feel for the state. My initial impression was based on my antipathy for the Dallas Cowboys: loud, boisterous fans and an owner with an ego the size of, ah, Texas. Sheryl and I spent 30 running days in the state; about 40 days total.

A LOOK BACK AT THE SCENERY DURING MY FIRST UPHILL CLIMB IN TEXAS.

I DID A DOUBLE TAKE AND STOPPED IN MY TRACKS WHEN I SAW THIS SIGN.

I crossed into Texas at Deweyville after running over a short bridge from Louisiana that crossed the Sabine River. As soon as I hit Texas soil, I knew it was going to be a fun run through the state. The roads' shoulders were very wide, the road itself was neat and clean, and I saw a lot of Texas flags and Lone Stars hanging in people's yards. Obviously, it is a very proud state. The murals along the interstate overpasses were beautiful works of art, with stars etched on the sides of each concrete support. I even passed a pond with an island in the shape of a star in the middle of the water.

Texas, to me, has two distinct parts; East Texas with a heavy population and large towns and cities, and West Texas with farm land, small towns, heavy winds, and sparsely populated areas. The scenery in both parts is magnificent. Also, a lot of history has been preserved and celebrated throughout the state.

SOUR LAKE IS THE BIRTHPLACE OF TEXACO OIL, NEARLY 110 YEARS AGO.

Texans are proud of their roots and heritage and have a strong sense of independence. I got the impression that people in this state could easily tell the rest of the country to take a hike and secede from the Union. They would have no problem being self-sufficient as an independent country.

Sheryl and I were able to experience real Texas hospitality and the culture of the old and new West. Here is just a sampling of what we were able to see and do while running through the great state of Texas.

MAGNIFICENT CASTLE NEAR MAGNOLIA, TEXAS.

I ran through Sour Lake, birthplace of Texaco Oil almost 110 years ago.

We spent an afternoon in Bellville at an authentic medieval castle.

I ran through Montgomery, birthplace of the Texas flag.

While I ran, Sheryl got to visit the Blue Bell Creamery in Brenham.

We celebrated the 1,000-mile mark in Giddings at the Giddings Downtown Restaurant.

In the town square of Decatur, we ate at Sweetie Pie's Ribeyes, the best rib eye and baked potato I've ever had.

LEDBETTER. TEXAS, GENERAL STORE, OPEN SINCE THE 1880S.

I stopped for a drink at Ledbetter's grocery store, open since the 1880s. The population of the town of Ledbetter in 2000 was a "healthy" 76.

We got to experience a small-town travelling summer carnival in Graham.

We hit Houston at the start of Passover and were privileged to spend the first and second nights with the Cantor and head Rabbi of the largest conservative synagogue in the U.S., Congregation Beth Yeshurun.

MOTHER'S DAY IN BUFFALO GAP, TEXAS.

We traveled back to the Sixties when we had Mother's Day lunch at The Café, in the very small town of Buffalo Gap, population 463.

We spent a couple of nights in Austin where we experienced 6th Street, the Driscoll Hotel, and the city's music scene.

We attended a UT-Oklahoma baseball game on campus. What a beautiful campus.

While in Abilene, we attended Heritage Days, an exposition of what the Old West was all about: rodeos, horses, boots, guns, cowboy hats, spurs, chuck wagons, and saddles. Thousands of Texans: cowboys in their pressed and creased blue jeans, big buckles, fancy shirts, and cowboy hats, and cowgirls in their tight blue jeans, boots, hats, fancy shirts, and a lot of bling.

THESE WIND TURBINES ARE HUGE AND MAKE AN EERIE SOUND AS THE WIND TURNS THE PROPELLERS.

TEXAS WAS EXPERIENCING ONE OF ITS WORST DROUGHTS EVER. I SAW NO RAIN ON MY RUN, AND THERE WERE MANY FIRES.

ANOTHER BEAUTIFUL DAY IN TEXAS.

I ran through the wind turbine capital of the country in Texas.

In Lubbock, we toured Texas Tech, a truly beautiful campus.

I experienced firsthand being caught in a very bad dust storm for two hours while running near Tahoka.

The state of Texas is huge. The entire land mass of New England can fit into the Central Plains Region of Texas where Lubbock is. But the most noteworthy feature of Texas was how nice and friendly the people were to Sheryl and me. Everywhere we went people were friendly and accommodating. In restaurants, hotels, and stores, and along the roads as I ran, we were amazed at the friendliness of the people.

The wide open spaces were magnificent, as were the huge wind turbines I saw around the Abilene and Central Plains area. Texas was experiencing one of the worst droughts in their history during my run. And later, when we were running in west New Mexico and Arizona we heard the news that there were hundreds of forest fires throughout Texas, especially around the Houston area.

I'm not so critical of the Dallas Cowboys or their fans any longer. I understand the state's enthusiasm for anything Texas. I now get it.

CHAPTER ②②② TWENTY-TWO

Inspiration on I-10 to California

I PASSED BOB WIELAND AS I HEADED TO CALIFORNIA ON I-10.
WHAT AN INSPIRATION FOR ME.

Throughout my run, I got quite a few emails and texts both from people I knew and from total strangers saying that I was providing inspiration for them. I never considered my run inspirational. I was having way too much fun so it felt strange to think I was actually inspiring others. I guess being inspired is in the eye of the one being inspired.

As I was approaching the California state border on I-10, I noticed a van on the shoulder of the road. There was something in front of it, but I couldn't make out any details except that it was close to the ground.

At first I thought something had fallen off a truck and that the van had stopped behind it. As I ran closer, I saw the object was moving and realized it was a man riding some sort of wheeled device. I wasn't wearing my glasses and it took me a few seconds to realize what I was seeing.

As it turned out, it was Bob Wieland, a large man who was peddling a three-wheeled cycle, not with his legs, which he no longer had, but with his arms. The van was his support vehicle. As I slowed to a stop in front of him, I got the full picture.

His pace was very slow but he was making progress. He stopped as I approached and I introduced myself. I held out my hand and as he reached for mine, I was surprised at how big and strong his was. His hand dwarfed mine as we shook.

I asked him where he was headed and he told me Washington, D.C. I told him I was headed to San Diego. He had started in Los Angeles and had an aide/assistant with him who was formerly homeless. As we talked, I could tell that what he was telling me was something he had spoken of hundreds of times before. He was very pleasant and soft spoken. I was in awe of his size, his accomplishments, and what he was presently doing. This man was a fighter and had more determination in his eyes than I have ever seen in my life.

Bob had "run" the Los Angeles marathon in about 174 hours in 2003. He was a four-time world record holder in bench press. He was the only double amputee to complete the Ironman Triathlon in Hawaii. On top of all that, Bob had walked across America on his arms, over 3,000 miles, taking three years and eight months to complete.

As Bob told me an abbreviated version of his life's story, I was amazed by his accomplishments. He was a Vietnam Vet who had lost his legs when he stepped on a live mortar shell during the war. He was a huge man—not fat, but muscular; a body builder.

This man had decided to embrace his handicap, to make a wonderful and inspiring life for himself and others. He was very proud of himself and with good reason. He invited me to the back of his van which was full of articles, books, and memorabilia of his life's work. He had taken it upon himself to devote his life to accomplishing and overcoming physical challenges that few could ever dream of doing as healthy, whole human beings. It was his mission in life to help and inspire others who needed a lift to lead happy and productive lives.

In 1989 Bob had completed the Washington, D.C., Marine Corps marathon and was presented the Most Inspirational Award. Coincidentally, I too was there, running my first marathon.

We said our good-byes and I began to run west again. I had a little extra bounce in my step. I felt good, really good. I felt inspired.

I looked Bob up online and have listed below some of his accomplishments. It was truly an honor to meet this man, even more so while running across the country.

- Four-time record holder in the bench press: 507 lbs.
- Strength and motivation coach with the Green Bay Packers
- 1994 People magazine's "Six Most Amazing Americans" in the past 20 Years
- 1995 "Most Courageous Man in America" by the NFL Players Association and Jim Thorpe Foundation
- Only double amputee to complete the Ironman Triathlon
- Completed the New York, Marine Corps, and Los Angeles marathons
- 2001 Vietnam Veteran Foundation "Man of the Year"

Mother's Day— The Café, Buffalo Gap, Texas

Since there could be no better mother for our kids than Sheryl, I felt bad that it was Mother's Day and we were nowhere near family to celebrate the day. I told Sheryl that I would take the day off from running and we'd tour Buffalo Gap for the day. Buffalo Gap is a small Texas town near Abilene known for its authentic historical

THE CAFÉ IN BUFFALO GAP WAS A MOTHER'S DAY DINNER WE'LL NEVER FORGET.

village that includes a town hall, jail, church, general store, blacksmith's shop, doctor's office, dentist's office, school, gas station, and a few other structures—15 to be exact—as part of the outdoor museum reflecting life in the late nineteenth century. The town has a population of 463. The Buffalo Gap Historic Village is the attraction of the area, with a small town area on the outskirts of The Village.

We got to the town around 11:30 a.m., assuming the Village would be open, but it didn't open for another half hour so we went into the town area and saw The Café, open for lunch.

This Café was a one-room diner, the type that I love to try. We were greeted by a woman who told us we could sit anywhere. We took a table against the wall, and I waited for the church crowd to begin their march in for Sunday Mother's Day lunch. I was not disappointed.

I mention this dining experience because most people will never experience what we did on this very special Mother's Day 2011.

One of the things I loved most about my run was being able to take a trip back in time to places that have seemingly stood still, and be able to experience, again, the slower moving, more relaxed condition of our country as it was in the Fifties and Sixties. Buffalo Gap and The Café provided exactly this.

As we sat waiting to be served, a gentleman sitting alone at the table next to us was brought his lunch in a take-out bag. He had been drinking a Coke while he waited and when Sandra, the waitress who also happened to be the owner, brought him his lunch, he asked if he could have a cup to take his remaining Coke with him.

She walked away and, looking back over her shoulder, told the man to bring the glass back the next time he came in. Sheryl and I just looked at each other. Her casualness and immediate positive response was so refreshing.

I realize this was a small thing, but the implications were huge. I saw trust, friendship, honesty, and a lack of concern for the potential loss of a piece of property. There was no question in my mind and, obviously, in the mind of the owner, that this man would indeed return her glass. What an amazing scene, especially in a world where so much value is placed on personal property and surrounded by mistrust of others.

The Café was beginning to fill up, and I noticed that the other "waitress" was, in actuality, a customer who noticed the owner was shorthanded. She just got up and began helping. She had interrupted her own dining experience to help out by waiting on tables.

The owner came over to take our order. The menu had a choice of two hamburgers, one regular and one giant. I asked her the difference. She told me to order the regular one because it was plenty and I wouldn't be able to eat the giant one. I smiled at Sheryl. This woman was telling me to spend less in her restaurant. I took Sandra's word for it, and Sheryl ordered the salad.

I asked her if she was shorthanded because almost every table was full now, and the helper/customer had sat down for a few minutes to finish her meal. Sandra told us that her employee had not shown up and she hadn't heard from her. She seemed unfazed about being shorthanded, and I was quite impressed, especially since a large party of 12 had just walked in. In keeping with the obvious protocol in this diner, the party of 12 began rearranging tables and chairs on their own to accommodate their group. This was done as if it was a daily occurrence. The helper/customer walked over to the table and took their drink orders and passed out menus.

A table of four adults and two kids had just completed their lunch. They saw that Sandra was busy so they picked up their used plates, glasses, and silverware, and casually took everything back to the kitchen and put them in the sink for later washing. One of the men got a wet cloth from the kitchen and wiped the table clean, ready for the next diners. Then they sat back down and waited for Sandra to bring them their check.

Sandra brought us our lunch and we began to eat. I mentioned to her that she could sure use some help. She told us that over the last weekend, 100 bikers had stopped for lunch as they were passing through town and she was supposed to have three waitresses working that day, but they didn't show up. She said everyone pitched in and all 100 bikers were attended to, ate happily, helped out, and left.

I can't remember a more pleasant dining experience. The food was terrific. The people were very friendly. The prices were embarrassingly low. And the chance to relive a calmer, more respectful and genuine era was priceless. I wanted to hang around the restaurant the rest of the day, but we had to get to the Buffalo Gap Historical Village. We did hang around for a while longer just to take in the experience. We left totally satisfied and thankful for small towns.

A Few Noteworthy Events

Over the course of my run, certain events stood out, and I still remember their significance. Every day brought new experiences and different perspectives. This chapter touches on just a handful of those specific incidents and memories.

Day 3—Outside Jacksonville we checked into a dumpy motel near Lake City. In jest I asked the gentleman at the desk if there were any discounts for someone running across the country. He gave me a small discount and then asked if we wanted a smoking or non-smoking room.

MY FATHER PASSED AWAY FOUR DAYS BEFORE HIS 93RD BIRTHDAY. I MADE IT BACK IN TIME TO BE WITH HIM.

Day 10—March 1st would have been my dad's 93rd birthday. He had passed away four days earlier. I spent the day running and remembering the good times.

Day 11—At the end of my run in Sneads, Florida, just past the Apalachee Correctional Institution, two large prison officials drove up to me and asked where I was going, what I was doing, and who was with me. I answered the questions and they left. My interest in seeing such a nice, well-kept prison must have given the impression that I was scoping out the place.

Day 15—At the 300-mile mark, around DeFuniak Springs, Florida. I really began

OUR FIRST CELEBRATION DINNER—1000 MILES ON DAY 50 AT GIDDINGS DOWNTOWN RESTAURANT IN GIDDINGS, TEXAS.

to feel strong and in shape. Other than the annoyance of blisters on my feet, I was really feeling good.

Day 20—Passing through Magnolia Springs, Alabama, I ran past a mobile home that had a Confederate flag waving in the front yard. I was surprised and a little ashamed that my home state still had dumb ass rednecks who refused to let go of the past and ignored the offensive symbolism.

From Jacksonville Beach through Houston, I noticed constant companions — buzzards. I could never figure out if they were telling me something or I just didn't realize what a fixture they were near the highway. In the desert areas, they were gone.

Day 26 — In Waveland, Mississippi, on Route 90, you'll see my signed dollar bill at the Seafood and Po'boys Drive-In. They were just getting the place set up when I stopped for a drink, and I was their first customer. They were kind enough to accommodate me, probably because I was wearing my Alabama hat, and the owner was a fan.

HOMELESS AND ON HIS WAY TO OREGON AFTER BEING REFUSED WORK BY A FRIEND.

Day 50 — I'll never forget finishing my run on day 50 — 1000 miles. I couldn't believe I had run that far. Then I realized I was not even half way to San Diego; a very brief letdown that was forgotten when Sheryl and I celebrated 1000 miles at the Giddings Downtown Restaurant.

Day 66 — The day after returning from our niece's wedding in Birmingham, I continued my run on Route 380, just west of Post, Texas. It started out as another beautiful day, sunny with mild winds. As the day progressed, the winds picked up and the dust began to blow. With about two hours to go, I was fighting 35 mph winds blowing dirt all around me. It was so bad that when I hit Tahoka, Texas, I had to seek shelter behind a wooden fence in someone's front yard. That's where Sheryl found me. I was covered in red dust.

Day 72 — I gave all my water to a homeless man who was walking to Oregon. He had walked from Oklahoma City, Oklahoma, to Lubbock, Texas, looking for work.

HORSES LET ME RUB THEIR FACES — COWS RAN AWAY FROM ME.

His friend in Lubbock saw that he had a brace on his leg and declined to give him a job. So he was on his way to Oregon for work. I felt bad for this man. He had a bum knee with a heavy brace on, and was walking and hitching rides to get to Oregon. He had no water or food when I saw him and he looked beaten down. All I had was my water and I gave it to him. It was the least I could do. He was in much worse shape than I.

Day 74—I encountered a couple and their four kids who had stopped to change a flat tire, just east of Ft. Sumner. I offered to help because the man had used the jack incorrectly and had to start over. He declined my help. I told him that there was an auto repair shop in Ft. Sumner on Route 60. I wished them well and left. A few miles down the road, they stopped beside me, handed me two bottles of water that a passing car had given them, and the kids waved to me as they headed to Ft. Sumner. They also were going to Oregon.

Day 79—I was running near Willard, New Mexico, and passed some prehistoric salt beds. When I hit the town of Willard, I was met by three little kids who were selling snow cones outside a closed gas station to raise money for their back-to-school clothes in the fall. Sheryl and I gave them $10 and we had terrific cherry snow cones.

THESE KIDS WERE SELLING SNOW CONES TO EARN MONEY TO BUY SCHOOL CLOTHES. LOVE CHERRY SNOW CONES!

Day 82—We spent two evenings with Jeff and Julia Baker, my nephew's future in-laws, in Albuquerque, New Mexico, and enjoyed a great home-cooked authentic New Mexico meal of fajitas made by hand by Julia. The best ever and our first taste of the famous New Mexico red and green peppers.

Day 87—When I was running in the area of Springerville, Arizona, we were hopping from one time zone to another. Our car's clock was stuck on Central Time, but I was running in Mountain Time, just before I entered Arizona. To spice up the time confusion even more, we were staying in a motel located in the Pacific Time Zone. It was confusing for a few days. On another note, we learned that Pie Town is one of the few places in the country where you can see the Milky Way.

THE CITIZENS OF SPRINGERVILLE AND EAGER, ARIZONA, SHOWED THEIR APPRECIATION TO THE FIREFIGHTERS WHO PROTECTED THEIR TOWNS FROM THE WILDFIRES BURNING OUT OF CONTROL.

Day 88—While staying in Springerville, Arizona, we saw a lot of signs in store windows and hung on fences thanking the firefighters for their hard work in fighting the Wallow Fire that had caused the town to evacuate the week before we got there. I've

THE HOMELESS PROBLEM ACROSS THE COUNTRY IS WORSE THAN ONE CAN IMAGINE.

A MAKESHIFT HOMELESS SHELTER WEST OF EL CENTRO, CA.

never seen a town so appreciative of help. Stores even advertised that there were discounts offered to all firemen who shopped with them.

Day 113—While running through the Imperial Valley during our stay in El Centro, California, I saw quite a bit of homelessness. It made me appreciate what I did have, and I felt so bad for those living on the streets. Passing shelters and men sleeping in the grass was heartbreaking.

THE CAFÉ IN BUFFALO GAP, TEXAS. A WONDERFUL EXPERIENCE!

AUTHENTIC CHUCKWAGON AT HERITAGE DAYS IN ABILENE, TEXAS.

KIDS ROPING EVENT DURING HERITAGE DAYS.

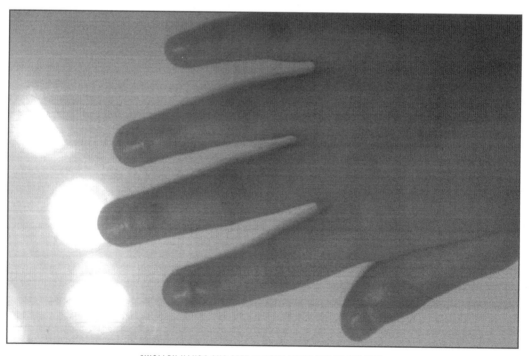

SWOLLEN HANDS AND FEET ALMOST EVERY DAY OF THE RUN.

TEXAS TECH UNIVERSITY IN LUBBOCK. BEAUTIFUL CAMPUS, MEDIOCRE FOOTBALL.

WINE VINEYARDS IN TEXAS. WHO KNEW?

MILES AND MILES OF OPEN FARM LAND IN TEXAS.

I PASSED HUNDREDS OF THESE OIL DRILLING MACHINES IN TEXAS.

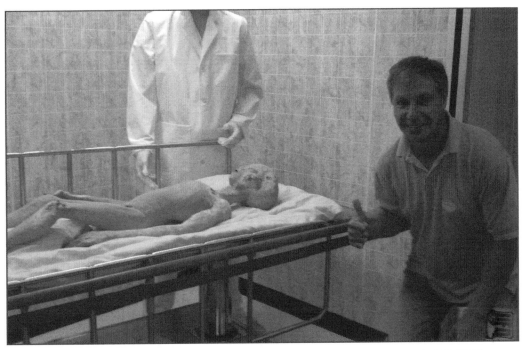

A VISIT TO THE HOSPITAL WHERE THE ALIENS ARE TREATED FOR INJURIES RECEIVED WHEN THEY CRASHED IN ROSWELL, NEW MEXICO IN 1947.

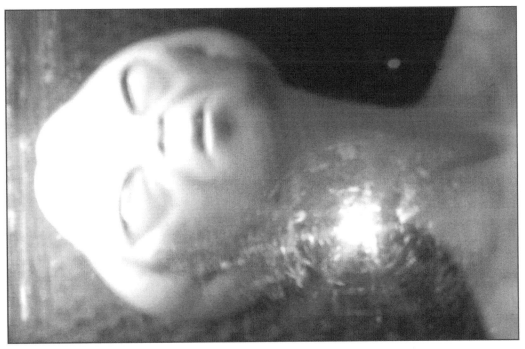

THE ALIEN, NAMED MELON, IS STILL IN A COMA SINCE THE 1947 CRASH.

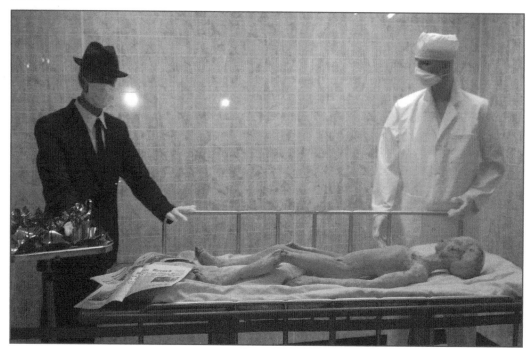

MEN IN BLACK ARE ALWAYS WATCHING WHEN GUESTS VISIT THE ALIENS.

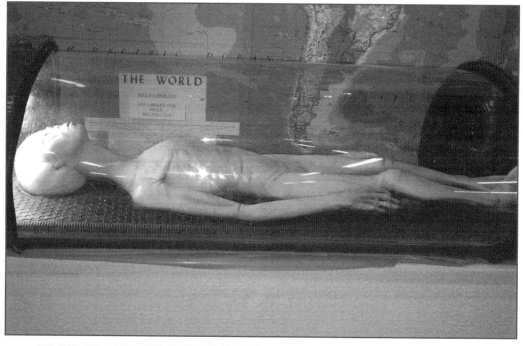

THIS ALIEN WAS BADLY INJURED DURING THE CRASH OF HIS SPACECRAFT IN 1947 NEAR ROSWELL, NEW MEXICO.

A MUST-SEE MUSEUM IF YOUR NEAR FT. SUMNER, NEW MEXICO.

HEADSTONE OF BILLY THE KID AND HIS PALS TOM O'FOLLIAD AND CHARLES BOWDRE.

A GREAT DAY OF RUNNING—WIDE SHOULDERS, LITTLE TRAFFIC.

I NEVER GREW TIRED OF WIDE OPEN SPACES AND SILENCE.

READY FOR MY RUN FOR THE DAY.

ENTERING TAIBAN, NEW MEXICO—POPULATION 7.

THE POST OFFICE IN TAIBAN, NEW MEXICO.

JOSEPH'S RESTAURANT. ONE OF THE ONLY ORIGINAL DINERS REMAINING ON THE FAMOUS ROUTE 66.

MY DAILY DROP-OFF WHERE I ENDED THE DAY BEFORE. MANY TRAINS TO WATCH AS I RUN THROUGH NEW MEXICO. A MASK DAY.
SMOKE IN THE AIR FROM THE FOREST FIRES IN ARIZONA.

ESTANCIA SALT BASIN NEAR WILLARD, NEW MEXICO.

COMING OUT OF THE MOUNTAINS AND HEADING TOWARD ALBUQUERQUE.

SHERYL RELAXING IN THE HISTORIC TOWN SQUARE IN SANTA FE.

CRYSTAL BLUE SKIES ALMOST DAILY. ONE DAY OF RAIN IN 119 DAYS OF RUNNING.

RUNNING FROM SOCORRO UP THE MOUNTAIN TOWARDS MAGDALENA AND THE VLA

LUNCH IN MAGDALENA, NEW MEXICO WITH DANIELLE, OWNER OF THE BEAR MOUNTAIN COFFEEHOUSE.

HEADING UP TO THE CONTINENTAL DIVIDE, OVER 7700 FEET. A LOT OF HUFFING AND PUFFING!

SMOKE IN THE AIR HEADING TOWARD SPRINGERVILLE, ARIZONA—EVACUATED THE WEEK BEFORE WE ARRIVED THERE.

DECORATED TREE ALONG ROUTE 60 HEADED TOWARD THE ARIZONA LINE.

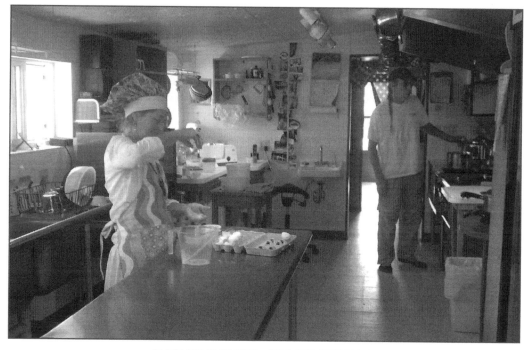

BAKING PIES IN PIE TOWN—PIE-O-NEER RESTAURANT.

EERIE SIGHT! ONE OF THE RADIO TELESCOPES IN THE VLA UNDER A HAZY MOON.

AN AMAZING SIGHT ON THE PLAINS OF SAN AGUSTIN. TOTAL SILENCE WITH A FEW DEER AND RABBITS RUNNING AROUND.

A PORT-A-JOHN IN THE MIDDLE OF NOWHERE HEADING TO QUEMADO, NM. WHERE WAS THIS 800 MILES AGO WHEN I REALLY NEEDED IT?

BEAUTIFUL, PEACEFUL ARIZONA HEADING TO SHOW LOW, ARIZONA.

MURAL IN DOWNTOWN SHOW LOW, AZ DEPICTING THE CARD GAME THAT DETERMINED WHO WOULD OWN THE TOWN.

EFFECTS OF YEARS OF FOREST FIRES IN ARIZONA.

A FEW NEVER PAY ATTENTION.

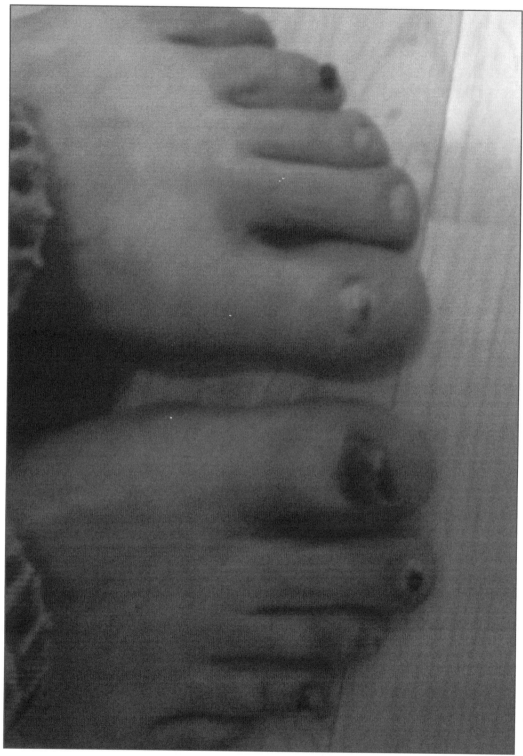

MY TOES SUFFERED THE WORST. MY DOGS WERE ALWAYS BARKING!
OVER 5,000,000 STEPS — 2,500,000 FOR EACH PUPPY.

ALWAYS A SIGHT FOR SORE EYES. ROAD CREWS WITH IGLOO WATER JUGS AND PLENTY OF ICE WATER. NO CUPS, JUST HANDS!

WHEREVER WE WENT, WE MADE FRIENDS. JULY 4TH IN SCOTTSDALE, AZ.

RUNNING ON I-10 FOR 100 MILES TO GET TO THE CALIFORNIA BORDER. THANK YOU ARIZONA STATE POLICE FOR GIVING ME A FREE PASS ON THE INTERSTATE!

LOOK, BUT DON'T DRINK. IRRIGATION CANALS THROUGHOUT ARIZONA.

RUNNING TOWARDS QUARTZITE, ARIZONA ON I-10. CALIFORNIA, HERE I COME! ONE DAY AWAY FROM MY 8TH AND FINAL STATE.

HOPPED THE FENCE AND RAN ACROSS THE COLORADO RIVER INTO CALIFORNIA.

MY FAVORITE MILE MARKER!

LUSH, GREEN FARMLAND WELCOMED ME TO CALIFORNIA.

HEADING INTO THE IMPERIAL SAND DUNES OUTSIDE GLAMIS, CA.

112 TO 114 DEGREES ALMOST EVERY DAY WHILE RUNNING IN SOUTHERN CALIFORNIA. THE IMPERIAL SAND DUNES. BEAUTIFUL, OPEN-AIR FURNACE.

TOUGH GOING ON THE FINAL STRETCH TO THE PACIFIC. ROUTE 78 TOWARDS GLAMIS, CA.

BARREN, DRY, HOT, AND I'M BEGINNING TO FEEL THE EFFECTS OF OVER 2200 MILES OF RUNNING.

PASSING MIRAMAR MARINE CORPS AIR STATION. WHAT A GREAT FEELING!!

FINAL 20 MILE RUN ENDING AT PACIFIC BEACH ON JULY 27TH . 2.3 MILES TO GO TOMORROW MORNING.

THANK YOU, SHERYL, I COULD NOT HAVE DONE THIS WITHOUT YOU!

MY FINISHERS SHIRT — RICHARD YOU DID IT. ROLL TIDE.

WITH FRIENDS AND FAMILY AFTER I TOUCHED DOWN AT CRYSTAL PIER AT PACIFIC BEACH, SAN DIEGO, CALIFORNIA.

Indian School Road Disaster

Considering all the running I did on this trip, having only two bad days wasn't bad at all. But those two days more than made up for their infrequency; they were really bad—and unforgettable.

The first bad day started out that way. I was west of Phoenix heading toward Tonopah, Arizona, on day 102, July 8. Usually I felt pretty good at the start of my runs,

A BUZZARD. THEY ACCOMPANIED ME THROUGH FOUR STATES.

both physically and mentally. I had no major injuries and I was looking forward to my day's run—4½-5 hours of being alone and just running. But this day, as soon as I started to run, I didn't feel right. I was struggling from the very first step and didn't know why.

I continued to run despite knowing it was going to be one of those 114-degree days in the blistering Arizona summer sun. I was on Indian School Road, according to the map.

After a few miles I got thirsty. I saw a small church on the right and, seeing that the parking lot was empty, I assumed it was closed. I figured I'd find the outside faucet and take a drink after letting the water run long enough to allow the burning hot water to be replaced by cooler water. I was wearing my water belt with two bottles of water, but I tried to conserve that and use other water sources if they became available along the way.

I found the faucet and took a drink. Normally I feel refreshed after drinking, especially water from a faucet or something other than the hot water on my belt. But today, the water did nothing to help relieve the heat and exhaustion I felt after running only a few miles.

I continued on my way, and suddenly a company truck pulled up beside me and a guy got out. He walked to the back of the truck and handed me two ice cold bottles of water. I must have looked pretty bad because he wasn't offering the water as a question; he was telling me to take the water. He wasn't going to take no for an answer, and I wasn't about to decline his help. I thanked him and stood for a few minutes drinking.

IRRIGATION CANALS RUNNING THROUGH PHOENIX.

This cold water made me feel a little better. I thanked him again and asked where the bridge that crossed I-10 to Tonopah was. He said it was about two miles ahead. I had already decided, for the first time on the run, I was going to cut my day short. I simply had no energy and the longer I was in the sun, the worse I was feeling. I had never before felt so bad during a run.

About ten minutes later, I was beginning to get lightheaded and felt faint. I tried to sit on the edge of a canal, but when I bent down, I almost passed out. Sitting made me feel even worse. I had gone about 14 miles and needed to make it to the I-10 ramp at Tonopah for Sheryl to pick me up. I could see the overpass in the distance.

As I was standing up again, the man who had given me water earlier pulled up alongside me. He asked if I was okay. I really must have looked as bad as I felt. He told me a farmer had just given him a box of cold cantaloupes. He 'told' me to sit in the truck and cool off.

ARIZONA—HOT! DAMN HOT! AND DRY!

I climbed into the truck and his partner turned the air conditioning on high and pointed all the vents toward me. It felt great and I started to feel better. The ice cold cantaloupe was as refreshing a snack as I have ever had. I sat for a while longer, took a few more drinks of cold water, thanked them again, and headed on. My goal after that was to make it to the truck stop at the Tonopah exit and call Sheryl. My body would not go farther that day.

As I trudged along, I saw the overpass I was seeking. At last the end was in sight. When I got closer to the exit, I saw the road made a dramatic curve away from the overpass which meant more distance between me and the truck stop. I had no choice but to plug along. I learned very early on in the run that there was absolutely nothing to gain from moaning and bitching about a no-options situation.

First, it would have been miserable. Second, it would have been physically draining. I just put my head down and very slowly jogged and walked on.

I finally reached the end of the road and turned left to begin the run on the overpass leading to the three gas station/convenience stores in Tonopah. I think this was all there was to the town. The overpass was arched so the first half was uphill. I just walked along trying to stay focused on making it a few hundred yards further. Coming down the other side, I also walked. I had no energy.

I finally reached the store and sat on the walkway for a few minutes. I was so weak I could barely get back up to go inside for a drink. By now the temperature was 115. I called Sheryl and told her where I was and that she needed to pick me up early. She asked if I was okay; I told her I was, but this was it for the day.

I went inside the store and was almost paralyzed by the cold. I went from 115 degrees to about 68 as I passed through the door. A few steps into the store I began to shake. I bought a drink and immediately left to sit outside and wait. As I sat there, I tried to determine why I felt so bad. It was hot, but the previous days in the heat had been fine.

When Sheryl picked me up, we drove right to Walmart where I got a Camelbak, a lightweight insulated backpack that holds 64 ounces of liquid. A plastic tube extends from the reservoir and serves as a straw to suck the liquid into your mouth. Sheryl was convinced I was suffering from dehydration, and she got no argument from me. From that day until the end of my run, I used the Camelbak.

I also decided, taking the advice of friends who are nurses, that I would shorten my runs for a few days until the temperatures lowered a bit. They emailed me and told me that I was indeed dehydrated and needed to slow down in these dangerously high temperatures. One nurse, Annie, told me to hydrate until my urine was clear, that this heat was nothing to fool around with.

For the first time on the run, I took this kind of advice seriously. I never wanted to feel like that again. I think that was the worst I had ever felt in my life.

On a good note, it did force me to buy a Camelbak, which I should have started using 100 miles earlier.

LIFE SAVING CAMELBAK. SECRET FORMULA: 2 PARTS GATORADE, 1 PART RUBY RED, ICE.

CHAPTER  26 TWENTY-SIX

Billy the Kid
and Historic Route 66

The only thing I knew about Billy the Kid was that he was a young outlaw in the Wild West. After running through Ft. Sumner, New Mexico, and staying there for four days, I know a lot more about this guy and the town where he died.

Ft. Sumner is a sleepy town that should be thankful every day to Billy the Kid for its very existence. If it weren't for him and the hoopla surrounding his death, which prompted a museum and an infamous burial site, this town would have blown away with the tumbleweeds years ago.

AN AWESOME OLD WEST MUSEUM. FT. SUMNER, NEW MEXICO.

The current population is about 1000, and Sheryl and I were ready to hang ourselves after the second day. Once you've seen the very neat museum and travel a little bit to see the burial site of The Kid and his pals a few miles from the museum, that's it—except for the Dairyland Drive-In, where we ate almost all of our meals. The town's folks were very nice, but four days here were two-and-a-half days too long.

But I will confess, the museum in the center of town (and next door to the motel we stayed in) is a must-see if you are ever within a 75-mile radius. At first glance, it's a small, quaint, very neat museum depicting the life, times, and death of Billy the Kid, and all that transpired before and after his stay in Ft. Sumner. But, as you round what appears to be the final corner of the museum, there is another section, then another, then another, until you have enjoyed two more hours in what appeared to be a very small, well defined exhibit.

This museum turned out to have a huge display of Old West exhibits, including a very large gun and rifle collection, Indian artifacts, military artifacts (from when Ft. Sumner was a military fort detailed to manage the Navajo and Apache Indian reservation), turn-of-the-century vehicles, early household tools and machinery, typewriters, clothing, and blacksmith paraphernalia. There was also a smaller museum and cemetery just outside of town where Billy the Kid and his pals, Charlie Bowdre and Tom O'Folliard are buried. The three friends lay side-by-side in the cemetery with a single, common headstone engraved with the word "Pals." The headstone had been stolen three times before the town put a steel fence around the plot.

1800S HEARSE AT THE BILLY THE KID MUSEUM FT. SUMNER, NEW MEXICO.

The other bright spot in the town was the Dairyland Drive-In. Located on the main drag, Route 60, diagonally across from our hotel, this small hamburger joint served as our dining oasis while in Ft. Sumner. Every day after I ran, we'd go there and eat lunch. It was so good we added dinner. As we dined, we got a chance to see the locals parade in and out. Since Sheryl and I, especially me in my running clothes, usually soaking wet, stuck out like sore thumbs, we got more than the casual glance from the town folk. But they were friendly enough and after they had their five-second stare at me, they went about their meal. The hamburgers and fries were incredible, and the milkshakes were like the old days, so thick you couldn't suck them through a straw. The prices were from 20 years ago, too! Great food, and cheap. Plus, the owner was as nice as could be.

After I had run as much as I could while staying in Ft. Sumner, we decided to head to Santa Rosa and experience another part of Americana that had been on my to-do list for years—we hit America's highway: Route 66.

Route 66 is the original highway from Chicago to Los Angeles, established in 1926. It passes through eight states and, today, some of the original motels and restaurants are still in operation along sections of the highway. For years, it was a goal of mine to travel the entire route from beginning to end. We didn't do that this trip, but we got a real feel for the experience while in Santa Rosa and Albuquerque.

Santa Rosa is still a small town, but three times the size of Ft. Sumner, with a population of less than 3000. The added plus was that for almost the same amount of money as the Super 8 Motel in Ft. Sumner we were able to stay at a "luxurious" Holiday Inn Express.

Route 66 passes right through Santa Rosa where many of the original motels and drive-ins are still operating. This was the highway that made the west accessible to everyone in the country, starting in the late 20s.

We stayed on Route 66 just a few hundred yards from the original strip where the motels and restaurants were. We ate at Joseph's Bar and Grill, The Comet II Drive-In, Route 66 Restaurant, and the Sun and Sand Restaurant. The food was just okay, but the atmosphere and the memorabilia were priceless. Joseph's logo, the "Fat Man," was seen on billboards on both sides of town. Back in the day, being a little fat was a

A COUNTRY CHURCH IN TEXAS, FOUNDED IN 1884.

sign of prosperity, thus the "Fat Man" image. It sure doesn't have the same meaning today.

We toured the Route 66 Auto Museum and saw the huge collection of beautiful classic cars of the 20s, 30s, 40s, 50s and 60s.

On the west end of town, Sheryl and I saw the railroad overpass that was in the film adaptation of John Steinbeck's The Grapes of Wrath. In the movie, Henry Fonda hops the train as it goes over the Pecos River Railroad Bridge.

We also visited the famous Blue Hole, also known as "Nature's Jewel." It's a crystal-clear diving hole in Santa Rosa, visited by divers from all over the world. For more than an hour, we watched divers go down exploring. It's about 80 feet wide and 80 feet deep. It widens at the bottom to about 120 feet. On the other side of the walkway is the stream where the clear water flows away from the Hole.

The best part of Santa Rosa was heading to the local high school to watch a Little League baseball game. The kids were probably 10 or 11. It was so nice to see the parents were all friends, and they were out there with their families enjoying the game. They cheered, but the overly competitive attitude you normally see was absent. There were no parents or coaches yelling at the kids or other parents, something I

PEOPLE FROM ALL OVER THE WORLD COME TO SCUBA DIVE IN THIS CRYSTAL CLEAR POOL IN SANTA ROSA, NEW MEXICO.

lived with for 25 years during my three kids' sports years. These were families there for friendship, not the outcome of the game. The kids took the game seriously but were not overly aggressive in their play.

The weather was perfect and it was a great way to relax and enjoy the local color while seeing small town kids and their families having a great time together.

It was a brief yet fun travel-back-in-time when family car trips included meals at diners and nights in neat motels where you could just drive up to your room, park, and walk in. There was even a TV series named "Route 66." Now, the restaurants are full of Route 66 memorabilia and just-fair food, and the motels are quaint, but you want to sleep in one only as a last resort. We noticed quite a few bikers in their 60s who possibly had the same idea I had; make the trip down memory lane before the drooling and senility set in. It must be a baby boomers' thing.

I was glad we had the chance to see parts of this historic roadway and experience what was once a big part of a great time and place for a lot of people traveling across the country. I was a little sad and disappointed to see its decline and fall from grace as I-40 and other interstates grew and overshadowed the charm of Historic Route 66. But I got my T-shirt as a reminder of the good time we had, and I will continue to picture Route 66 as I suppose it once was.

CHAPTER **27** TWENTY-SEVEN

Alien Nation— Roswell, New Mexico

For 40 years I've been fascinated by the whole idea of aliens, spaceships, close encounters, and especially Roswell, New Mexico. As far as I am concerned, Roswell is the center of the alien nation universe.

The Roswell UFO mystery is, arguably, the most famous of all alien tales in America. According to folklore, on July 8, 1947, a UFO with crew on board crashed near Roswell. The aliens were supposedly taken to a government facility, and the entire episode was covered up by our government. The cover-up included a story originating from the government that a weather balloon had crashed.

With UFO sightings growing in the 1940s, coupled with the narrative told by the farmer who purportedly found the UFO, the story has become one of the greatest unsolved mysteries in American history.

Before my run took us to New Mexico, beginning in Texico, I had never really spent any time in the state. I had just briefly passed through New Mexico when I drove our daughter to her new job in San Diego. On that trip we passed through Las Cruses, home of New Mexico State University.

When Sheryl and I looked at the map of New Mexico, with only a few running days remaining in Texas, I was disappointed to find that I would not be able to run through the town of Roswell. There were virtually no motels from the Texas/New Mexico border to Roswell; almost 100 miles and nowhere to sleep. Therefore, my route had to be farther north where towns were closer together and had reasonable accommodations.

So from Plains, Texas, we had to make our way due north in order to continue my run on Route 70 just outside Muleshoe, Texas. That turned into Route 60 when I crossed into New Mexico at the small border town of Texico.

There was no way I was going to be that close to Roswell and not check it out. Fortunately, I finished my run to Plains on a Friday, so we were able to drive up to Clovis, New Mexico, to spend a few days, as I ran through that area. Our plan was to drive to Roswell on Saturday, my non-running day, and visit the alien museum and all the tourist traps I assumed were in town. I was not disappointed.

That Saturday we made the 110 mile drive from Clovis to Roswell. As we entered the city we immediately began seeing big green alien figures in front of stores, along the streets, and tied to fences. I was getting more and more excited with each alien we passed.

ONE OF THE ORIGINAL MOTELS ON HISTORIC ROUTE 66, SANTA ROSA, NEW MEXICO.

We drove into the downtown area where the UFO Museum was located, paid for tickets, and entered the world of Roswell UFO mania. If you enjoy the subjects of UFOs, aliens, and government cover-up conspiracies, you may want to put the Roswell UFO Museum on your "to-do" list. There are original artifacts from the crash area, police and government reports, affidavits from local, military, and government sources, original pictures, and detailed explanations of what actually happened that July day in 1947 on Marc Bruzel's farm outside Roswell.

If you're like me and enjoy thinking of the possibilities of visits from aliens, this is the place to indulge your fantasy. Based on the exhibits, one can leave with a very strong opinion that there was, in fact, an alien spaceship crash near Roswell. If you are a terminal skeptic and always keep your feet planted firmly on the ground, you can also walk away thinking this is just another sensational hoax. If nothing else, you can leave satisfied that you got to see the epicenter of one of the most talked about, publicized, and researched events involving extraterrestrial possibilities. Even my wife, who is as level-headed as anyone I know, was not so sure anymore that what was reported was not, in fact, real.

Another dream come true, this visit to Roswell, New Mexico. It was better than I had expected. We both left satisfied that the possibilities of fact were a shade greater than the possibilities of fiction.

A bonus, as we headed out of town on our 110-mile drive back to Clovis, was that we found a gas station and paid only $3.16 a gallon. Everywhere else, both in Roswell and for the entire Transamerica trip, gas was $3.69 to $3.89 a gallon. We hadn't seen gas that cheap for months and never saw it that cheap again. It must have been an alien thing.

CHAPTER **28** TWENTY-EIGHT

The Return of the Sheriff

Other than one incident with a local Texas police officer, my experiences with law enforcement officers throughout my run were all good. My experience with one Texas deputy sheriff was exceptional.

On a fine running day in Texas, near Graham, on day 56 to be exact, I was plugging along as usual. It was one of many days that I just felt great. I had no worries or responsibilities except my promise to Julie that I would be hugging her as we stood in the Pacific Ocean.

As I ran, I looked up and saw a police vehicle heading right toward me. I froze and watched the truck coming steadily closer, ready to jump into the grass in case it didn't change direction. When it got about 30 yards away it swerved back onto the road and passed me.

I stood on the shoulder and watched as it passed me and headed down the road. I put my hands on my hips and watched it as it went over the hill and out of sight. I said to myself, "Why the hell is a deputy trying to scare me off the road? I expect that kind of thing from rednecks and white trash, but from a police officer? What is this all about?"

I continued running, annoyed that this law enforcement person tried to ruin a good run. Just as I finished that thought, the vehicle passed me again with lights flashing. I immediately felt nervous. It went on for about 50 yards and then made a U-turn and headed back toward me.

Now I'm thinking, This cop is going to arrest me for giving him the stinky eye when he passed me. I decided to put my arms out to my side so he wouldn't think I was in any way a threat. As absurd as that sounded in my head, I wasn't going to take any chances considering I was dealing with a law enforcement officer who'd just tried to scare me off the road.

As the deputy approached me, I realized that he was actually a she. Now I thought that I was probably dealing with a ball-busting female deputy. I was envisioning her getting out of the truck, hand-cuffing me and accusing me of flipping her off as she passed me.

She pulled her vehicle up next to me, as I remained motionless, got out, and said, "I am so sorry for doing that. My radio went off and I looked down to pick it up. I lost

175

control of the truck for a second. I am so sorry." I was shocked and relieved at the same time. My fear of needing to call Sheryl to get me out of jail disappeared.

I told her that it was no problem, not to be concerned. I said how much I appreciated her coming back to explain, that it had seemed a little odd. She dug into the ice chest in the back of her truck and offered me two bottles of cold water. We spoke for a few minutes and she asked me what I was doing out there. She wished me well, we shook hands, and I thanked her again for her kindness. I waved as she drove away. She waved back.

When was the last time a police officer apologized to you? All was right with the world again and I continued toward San Diego.

CHAPTER **29** TWENTY-NINE

Taiban, Yeso, Glamis

There's something appealing about a small town with its historic town square, old-time drug store and soda fountain, hamburger joint, mercantile, war memorials, and white-painted churches. It is Americana at its best. The locals are friendly and love to talk about the significance of their town and its famous or infamous historical tidbits.

Before my run, I had never been in towns with populations fewer than ten. I thought towns declaring a few hundred lived there were small, but less than that? I didn't even know towns like that existed.

I passed through three towns with populations fewer than ten. I was under the gross misconception that all towns had at least three entities: a church, a post office, and a market. I was wrong.

For Taiban, New Mexico, population seven, and Yeso, New Mexico, population six, it was a different story. I felt I was witnessing towns in the last throes of life.

My first "tiny" town was Taiban. As I approached the town, I saw no movement, no activity except a dog barking at me from behind a fence. On my left was a small, well-kept house with this barking dog and at least two cats. A few other structures in the immediate area were old, dilapidated, and abandoned. A car passed me and I saw it turn right. As I got closer I saw that the car had pulled into the small parking lot at the local post office.

When I stopped at the post offices in Taiban and Yeso, I noticed they were small and almost identical in design. I assumed that for these small towns—and growing smaller—the postal service had a neatly packaged architectural blueprint that allowed the town to have its own post office while not costing the taxpayers much money.

The postmasters, both women, told me that it was only a matter of time before budget cuts would shut them down. It felt like the women were waking up each morning waiting for the hammer to fall. They weren't distraught over the prospect of losing their jobs; they seemed resigned to the inevitable. Each was very nice and enjoyed seeing my surprise when they told me about the census count of the town. I got a drink from the outside faucet in Taiban and a warm Gatorade from the postmistress in Yeso.

As I ran out of each of these two towns, I tried to envision active, living municipalities of years past, with people in the streets, stores with open doors, and dogs barking at passing cars. But the reality was much different; there were only closed doors and weather-worn wood structures—their purposes unrecognizable--eerie silence (except for a barking dog), and they were one ghost short of being a ghost town. They will probably soon join Red Hill, New Mexico, the last ghost town on Route 60 before crossing the Arizona border.

I remember passing through Red Hill. I stopped in front of a small building to tie my shoe; there was nothing but a cat close to the road. A few hundred yards behind it was

a sign telling me that I was indeed in Red Hill. It was sad to see these towns at the back end of their lives.

GLAMIS, CALIFORNIA.

Glamis, California, a little northeast of El Centro, with a population of seven in the off-season, was a different story.

The main town dude, a fulltime resident of Glamis, gave me the lowdown on the town. It's a resort town without an ocean. Located in the Imperial Sand Dunes, the attraction is its pristine sand dunes that draw dune buggy enthusiasts in the winter. The summer, when I was passing through, is so hot that it's a ghost town. It consisted of the store where you rent buggies, get food, and just hang out, and a trailer, maybe where that guy lived. It was a beautiful setting, and if I were into dune buggies, I'd come back for the fun.

PEACE AND SOLITUDE ON THE PLAINS OF NEW MEXICO.

I'm not sure where the other year-round residents lived. I didn't see anything that resembled a residence of any kind, unless they all shared that one trailer, which, come to think about it, wouldn't be a shock.

I stopped at the little market to get a drink before heading into the blistering wind blowing across the beautiful scorched sand dunes. A state trooper passed me but then turned around. He pulled up beside me and crept along, keeping up with me as he asked if I was okay. I gave him the usual, "My wife is picking me up just down the road." He moved on, and I moved on into the furnace heat.

Glamis will survive as long as the sand dunes survive. I'm not sure about the other two. How would you feel if you met someone, told him where you were from, and then had to add, "But it's not there anymore"?

CHAPTER **30** THIRTY

VLA—Very Large Array

All of the amazing beauty I experienced on my run was natural: mountains, desert, crystal blue skies, rivers, lakes, and foliage. All that is, but one. Just west of Magdalena, New Mexico, on the flat Plains of San Agustin stood a perfectly aligned Y-shaped array of 27 radio telescopes called the VLA, or the Very Large Array. This

A VLA RADIO TELESCOPE ON THE PLAINS OF SAN AUSTIN BETWEEN MAGDALENA AND DATIL, NEW MEXICO.

radio astronomy observatory investigates astronomical objects such as the Milky Way, black holes, quasars, pulsars, stars, and planets. Each arm of the Y is about 13 miles long. The Y crosses Route 60, the road I ran on through most of New Mexico and into Arizona.

The area was perfectly flat with no trees. It felt eerie as I passed through the Y. It was very quiet with practically no traffic. A few deer ran past me trying to get back inside the fence that bordered Route 60. I stopped a few times and just stared at the scene. These huge satellite dishes are angled to face into space. Their purpose is to "listen" to invisible information about our universe. This man-made technology was such a visual contrast to the natural environment in which it was placed that it was jarring and "other worldly."

What was so amazing to me was how large the satellite dishes were. They were about 80 feet in diameter, and when I thought I was only a few hundred yards away, it took me about 20 minutes to reach the first one. It was only when I finally reached the dish closest to the road that I saw a railroad track ran alongside each of the dishes. This allows the satellites to be reconfigured and their angles to be adjusted. In the distance, south of the road as I headed west, was a very large building where the antennas are built and repaired.

LOTS OF OPEN SPACE IN NEW MEXICO.

If you saw the movie Contact, with Jody Foster, you saw the VLA, even though it was described as SETI, Search for Extraterrestrial Intelligence. It is not uncommon for most people to confuse the VLA with SETI. (SETI's mission, different from the VLA's, is to explore the universe for signs of life.) VLA was also used in the films Armageddon and Independence Day, among others.

During the filming of Contact, members of the Magdalena community, the town just east of the VLA, were used as extras in the movie. It was pretty neat to run past this area, realizing that it is well known and that people from all over the world come to the Plains just to see the VLA.

Information about the VLA and the area was provided by Danielle, the owner of the Bear Mountain Coffee Shop, where you will find the best tuna on toast in all of New Mexico. Danielle also called ahead to her friends in Springerville, Arizona, to get us updates on the Wallow Fire and available accommodations. Thanks, Danielle.

CHAPTER **31** THIRTY-ONE

Fire and Smoke

....

For me, New Mexico was broken into two parts; the New Mexico of high winds and some mountains east of I-25, and the New Mexico of winds, inclines, 7500 foot altitudes, flies, and smoke, west of I-25.

We started to hear about the fires when we were in Ft. Sumner, about a week before we stayed in Moriarty, New Mexico. When we got to Moriarty, the smoke from the fires was getting heavy and started to become a problem for me. We kept watching the news and continually heard reports that the Wallow Fire, as it was named, was spreading rapidly and heading directly into the path I was planning to run.

SMOKE PREVENTION MORIARTY, NEW MEXICO.

When we got to Moriarty, we found a town cloaked in a cloud of smoke and a nauseous smell. It is never a good sign when you can see the air you're breathing. The air quality was so bad that I bought surgical masks to wear as I ran. Even at night in the hotel I had to wear one. I remember lying in bed breathing through a surgical mask. To say that sleeping with a mask was uncomfortable is an understatement.

I remember Moriarty for the smoke we had to contend with and the continual news coverage about Congressman Weiner. There was nothing to do in Moriarty so we watched the Weiner collapse and paid attention to the weather reports that tracked the path of the Wallow Fire and its smoke.

As we approached Belen, New Mexico, right at I-25, we could see the clouds of smoke in the air. When

SMOKE-FILLED SKIES OVER BELEN, NEW MEXICO.

we checked into our hotel in Belen, we met a group of firefighters who had just checked in as well. I asked them about the direction of the fire and they told us that it was heading toward Springerville/Eagar, Arizona, right on Route 60. This was where we were supposed to stay as we entered Arizona. I was concerned, but not overly much because we had about a week before we reached that area and I decided I wasn't going to worry about it until I had to.

We used Belen as our home base while I ran through Encino, Lucy, Willard, and Mountainair, New Mexico. My concern during this time was that each day I had to run with a surgical mask. As I ran and breathed in, the fabric of the mask pressed against my mouth restricting my airflow. I had to change the shape of my lips to block the mask from being sucked into my mouth. It was a real pain. I certainly didn't want to remove it and be exposed to any long term effects from the putrid smoke I was breathing.

The problem in this locale wasn't fire but the winds that were blowing the smoke into the area. When I was finished running that Friday, we made plans to meet our

FIREFIGHTER IN BELEN, NEW MEXICO, WAITING TO FIND OUT WHICH SECTION OF THE WALLOW FIRE TO FIGHT NEXT.

friends Jeff and Julia Baker for dinner in Albuquerque, just north of Belen. During our visit, Jeff took out a map of New Mexico to see if we could find a more northerly route into Arizona, bypassing the smoke and fire. The reports on the fire and its lack of containment at that point were not good.

Jeff recommended that I take a route north through Flagstaff. As I examined the map, I realized that would put me in a lot of mountainous territory. I don't mind running uphill but I do mind the higher elevations and the overlooks into nothingness hundreds of feet down. Those exposed heights scare the hell out of me. Using what tact I could muster, I told Jeff that sounded like a feasible alternative route, but I'd rather take my chances along the fire and smoke line.

After Belen, we moved into Socorro to stay while I ran west of I-25, through Socorro, Magdalena, Datil, Pie Town, Quemado, and Red Hill, and into Arizona. When I hit Magdalena we ate at The Bear Mountain Café and struck up a conversation with the owner, Danielle. I told her we were headed to Springerville and asked if she had any current information on the evacuation of that town. She called a friend in Springerville to find out the latest, and informed us that the residents of Springerville and Eager were "possibly" going to be able to return to their homes in a day or two because the fire was being contained. Contained meant that the firefighters were able to encircle a portion of the fire with enough downed trees that the fire would not spread outside the containment. It certainly didn't mean they had put the fire out. At the time we were in Magdalena, the fire had burned over 530,000 acres. At its peak, the fire consumed over 800,000 acres of forest. It grew to be the largest forest fire in Arizona history. The strong winds had taken the smoke as far north as Minnesota.

Danielle said that the firefighters had blocked that part of Route 60 that crossed the Arizona border from New Mexico, right where we were going. That night Sheryl

THE DEVASTATION OF FOREST FIRES IN THE ARIZONA WILDERNESS.

called a few hotels in the Springerville area; some were closed, but she got an answer at the Rode Inn. The owner told Sheryl that all the rooms were booked by firefighters at the moment. She suggested we check back as we got closer to see if anything opened up. She said she already had a waiting list and offered to add our name, which she did.

We decided to keep running toward the town and take our chances. Sheryl told the woman what we were doing and said we'd sleep anywhere; we just needed a roof over our heads.

After I passed the VLA (Very Large Array), about 115 miles (six running days) from Springerville, we called the Rode Inn. The woman gave us a room, barring another evacuation, so we drove from Albuquerque to Springerville, about 230 miles. We used Springerville as our home base for 4 days as I ran the last 80 miles in west New Mexico and the first 20 miles in Arizona. From all reports on the local news and weather, we would be able to stay in Springerville and run until we were north and west of the fire and smoke.

The dodging of the Wallow Fire caused us to have to drive hundreds of miles a day back and forth for a few days, just so I could run 20 each day. While staying in Socorro we had to drive west on Route 60 for drop-offs and pick-ups until I hit Pie Town, New Mexico. Then when we were based in Springerville, we drove east to drop me and pick me up until I was passed Springerville and the smoke. The next stop was Show Low, Arizona.

I figured if we could just get to Show Low, Arizona, we'd be good to go. Show Low would put us north and west of the smoke and fire, and the winds were continually blowing north and east.

We stayed in Springerville for four nights as I completed my run through New Mexico and into Arizona. The benefit of staying at the Rode Inn during this time was that each morning we were able to get an update on the fires and smoke. Before I ran every morning, Sheryl and I went into the motel office and looked at the huge topography map the firemen used in their daily briefings. It was Greek to us, but I was able to check the direction of the winds and ask about the status of the fire containment. Also, the hotel provided me with a better quality mask every day. In addition to spare tooth brushes or extra soap, they gave out top quality surgical masks. What else could you ask for?

WALLOW FIRE MAP LOCATED IN THE RODE INN LOBBY WAS UPDATED DAILY.

We were grateful to have a room at the Rode Inn. It was our only non-branded hotel on the trip and although very nice and clean, we looked forward to being in Show Low, a much larger town. It even had a movie theater ($3.50 matinees).

We spent a few days there as I ran through Show Low, Linden, Heber/Overgaard, and Forest Lakes on Route 260. Just as I was entering Show Low, we got word that a new fire had started in Heber/Overgaard. I shook my head and decided that this must be normal for this part of the country and I wasn't going to worry about it. If I could make it past Springerville and the huge fire and smoke in that area, I didn't have to worry about a puny fire in the Heber/Overgaard area.

As a point of information: there seemed to be a few areas that were named for sister towns like Heber and Overgaard. They are two completely separate towns, but they are so close they are known by one name. The same was true for two towns south of Show Low: Pinetop/Lakeside.

The stretch of road in New Mexico on Route 60 between Mountainair and Red Hill was beautiful, but on top of the wind, forest fire smoke, mountains, and heat, the real annoyance was the horse flies that buzzed around me for over a week. I finally realized that it was probably my sweat that was attracting the flies, or maybe the sweet smell of my sunscreen.

In any event, it was so bad that in addition to sunscreen, I had to spray fly repellent on my face and neck every morning when Sheryl dropped me off. I even tried Deet, the repellent that is supposed to be the best for outdoorsmen, to ward off insects. Nothing worked. Each day's run was filled with swatting at flies, shaking my head, and even changing speed—anything to get away from the swarming flies.

If someone had driven alongside me while I was on this stretch of road, and observed my avoidance behavior with the flies, they would have thought I had numerous tics and was into masochistic slapping and hitting myself. On a positive note I did become skilled at holding my hand out, waiting for a fly to light, then swatting it. It was a sad state of affairs when my day's entertainment was killing flies and keeping count.

As quickly as they appeared, they faded away. Back to the pleasures of just running.

CHAPTER **32** THIRTY-TWO

I-10 State Trooper—Not Cool!

The run on I-10 from Tonopah, Arizona, to Blyth, California, was a last resort. I had had a horrible day leading up to my reaching the Tonopah exit. The intense heat, 105 to 114 degrees every day in that area was beginning to get to me. When Sheryl picked me up at the truck stop, we made two decisions immediately. First, Sheryl said we were going to Walmart to get the Camelbak I mentioned earlier, and I decided that I had had enough of the road problems in western Arizona; I was switching to the most direct route to the border—I-10. Roads like the Tonopah-Salome Highway and Indian School Road on a map looked like normal, passable roads to run on, but the reality was that The Tonopah-Salome Highway was a dirt road and the Indian School Road just came to a stop in the middle of nowhere. I found this out the hard way.

I was frustrated with searching for passable routes so I decided to take my chances with the state police and just run on the shoulder of the interstate. As we pulled away from Tonopah, I looked back to figure out where Sheryl would drop me off on Sunday to get onto the interstate. I realized all she had to do was go back to the truck stop we had just left and I would start my run going up the eastbound off-ramp and onto the eastbound side of the highway. Simple enough.

That next run, on Sunday, July 10, Day 103, I was feeling good and on my back was my brand spanking new Camelbak. My liquid concoction was four small bottles of Gatorade mixed with two small bottles of Ruby Red grapefruit juice. Plus, I loaded in ice since the Camelbak was insulated. I developed this special formula to satisfy my need for all the sugar and electrolytes Gatorade offers and the additional sugar and flavor from the grapefruit juice. Because of the huge amounts of Gatorade I consumed earlier in the run I was sick of it, regardless of the flavor. But I also knew that in the heat I needed the nutrients, so I masked the taste with the grapefruit juice. It worked beautifully. That became my drink of choice until I finished the run. It also stayed cold for a good four hours. The need to drink the nasty warm—bordering on hot—water from my water belt was over.

Sheryl dropped me at the truck stop at the Tonopah exit, and I went up the exit ramp of I-10. At first it felt strange being on the interstate on foot. Unless you are broken down or stopped by a state trooper, I don't think many people experience what it's like being on foot along an interstate highway. I thought that since I was in desolate western Arizona, the traffic would be light, but it wasn't. I-10 is the main highway from Los Angeles to Jacksonville, Florida. I had never seen so much truck traffic up close and personal. Fortunately, the shoulder is very wide, and I managed to run on the far edge of it.

I-10 BETWEEN TONOPAH, ARIZONA, AND THE CALIFORNIA BORDER. NICE WIDE SHOULDERS WITH HEAVY TRAFFIC AT TIMES, AND FENCING 30-40 YARDS OFF THE ROAD.

After about an hour of running, and noticing how many tractor trailer rigs were on the road, I saw my biggest I-10 nightmare: a state patrol car. Even worse, he was parked on the shoulder giving a driver a ticket. I thought of getting off the shoulder and walking behind him unnoticed, but I also figured he may have seen me in the distance and getting caught trying to sneak around him wasn't a good idea.

I decided to keep running. As I approached him, he didn't seem to notice me; he was intent on his conversation with the driver. I didn't want to surprise him so I made some noise as I approached. It didn't work. He was startled to suddenly see a man standing there with no other vehicle in sight. He seemed at a loss for words so I said, "Hi, I'm just running to San Diego." He stared at me and then in a business-like, but courteous tone, told me to wait for him by his car, which I did.

After a few minutes he finished with the driver, giving him a warning. I took that as a good sign, a state trooper with a heart. He walked over to me and asked if I knew that running on the interstate was illegal. I told him I called the Arizona Highway Patrol while still in New Mexico, and the person I spoke with told me that it was okay to run on the interstate. (It did surprise me that the person told me it was okay, but I accepted what he said as being correct, maybe because I wanted so desperately to believe him.) He said that I was given incorrect information. I said I was running on behalf of two charities and that I couldn't find any other suitable route to exit the state and enter California. I said if he could tell me of a road that wasn't on the maps, I'd be glad to run on it. My credible sob story.

He seemed to understand and told me that I could run on the interstate as long as his office didn't receive too many calls about a guy on the interstate. I asked if he did get calls, could I run on the other side of the fence (a wire fence on both sides of the interstate, about 20 yards from the shoulder. Not seen in the picture of I-10 on previous page). He replied that the interstate property extended only to the fence and not beyond. I guess this was his way of saying he had jurisdiction only up to the fence, meaning I could do what I wanted on non-interstate property.

That was all I needed to hear. I figured that if he had to kick me off the interstate, I would just hop the fence and run, as difficult and uncomfortable as that would be. At least I had a direct route to California. I thanked him, and off I went.

During the next few days, a few troopers passed me but did not stop. I wondered if the first trooper had alerted the others about what I was doing or if they simply didn't care.

On day 104, I was cruising along when I saw flashing blue lights in the distance. I figured there was no way the officer had seen me, so I got off the shoulder and down into a gully that was filled with bushes, trees, and dirt. I casually walked along. I didn't want it to look like I was trying to hide just in case he did stop. I'll be damned if the trooper didn't pull over where I was. When I saw him, I scurried up the embankment so he wouldn't think I was trying to avoid him, which is exactly what I was doing. I got to the top and immediately walked up to his passenger window. He leaned toward me and asked if I was attached to any vehicle. I told him my wife was coming in a few minutes to pick me up, that I was running to the California border. I said she was going to call me when she passed under the exit 69 overpass.

Then he said, "I just got a call that a car has rolled over just under the 69 overpass, maybe that's her. I gotta go." He sped off, leaving me utterly stunned. As I ran across the road, I saw the trooper speeding off with lights flashing and siren blaring. I fumbled for my phone and called Sheryl.

When she answered, I asked if she was okay. She said, "Yes. Why?" I told her I'd tell her when she got there. She was just passing under the overpass and said she'd pick me up in a minute.

I was running west, and she was driving east to west coming from The Wigwam. After she picked me up, we headed back east toward The Wigwam for our final night at the resort. As we approached Exit 69, I saw what Sheryl had just passed — the trooper along with ambulances and cars pulled off to the side of the road. In the middle of the scene was, indeed, an overturned car. Fortunately it didn't appear that there were any serious injuries. Sheryl must have been only a mile or two behind the car that turned over. I don't think the trooper realized how much he scared me.

CHAPTER **33** THIRTY-THREE

Phoenix/Scottsdale

··

As I ran through Globe and Superior, Arizona, in the mountains just east of Phoenix, I was getting my first experience of intense summer heat in the desert. On my last day in the mountains, before heading into the valley, Sheryl and I dropped off

HEADING TOWARD PHOENIX FROM THE MOUNTAINS NEAR SUPERIOR AND GLOBE.

two bottles of water at what would be mile markers 7 and 14 of that day's run. We did this as we drove east to my starting point for that day. We had left Globe and driven to Scottsdale to begin our stay, west of where I was running, thus the need to head east for a few days for me to be dropped off to run west. We dropped them at the mile markers so they would be easy for me to find.

I began my run around 7:30 a.m. and was feeling pretty good because we had stayed at a really crappy motel in Globe the night before and for the next few days we were moving our base to Scottsdale, where we were staying at a hotel with suites. By comparison, we were heading into the lap of luxury.

Someone asked me in Phoenix if I got up really early to run since the temperatures in the area were so high. I decided to keep to my regular time schedule, even in the blistering heat, for two reasons. First, I had heard that serious runners and bikers would get started at about 3-4 in the morning in order to beat the heat, and I wasn't going to lose valuable sleep to do that. Second, it was still dark that early, and I didn't want to risk injury running in the dark. It was too easy to misstep or get hit by a car because the driver couldn't see me. I was content to get started between 7:30 and 8:00 a.m., even though the temperatures were already in the 90s by then.

I began my descent into the valley and stopped at the first water drop. I easily found the full bottle of water. I hopped over the steel barrier and picked it up. The plastic bottle was so hot I could barely hold it. I opened the cap and took a sip. I had to leave the bottle there because the water was so hot it scalded my throat as it went down. So much for that bright idea. This was before I had gotten my Camelbak, still 100 miles farther on in Tonopah. My run would have been so much easier if I hadn't been

COOL AND COMFORTABLE WITH A SHORT SLEEVE SHIRT WORN OVER A LONG SLEEVE SHIRT.

so stubborn about carrying something on my back.

I continued running with the utterly stupid idea that the next water drop would be different. It was. The bottle was so hot at the 14-mile mark that I couldn't even pick it up. I just left it on the ground. I did have my water belt, but after a couple of hours in the 114-degree heat, even that water was hot and nasty. I used it only when absolutely necessary.

The good thing about my two-shirt system, a short sleeve T-shirt over a long sleeve T-shirt, was I stayed relatively cool during my runs because the long sleeve shirt was always soaking wet and cool under the short sleeve shirt. The only body discomfort and annoyance in this blistering heat was sweat and salt in my eyes. I always had a hard time figuring out why runners, in very hot weather, run without a shirt. My two-shirt system worked like a charm. Plus, I love running in the heat. I'm usually good for up to 105 degrees.

Running on Route 60 West had been a good road for me. The shoulders were wide and the scenery was magnificent, but when I looked at the map to see how to navigate Phoenix and the surrounding area, I saw that 60, at its approach to Mesa, became a major highway, almost like an interstate.

I decided to take the Old West Highway to Apache Junction and from there run on surface streets through the Mesa, Tempe, and Phoenix areas. We actually stayed north in Scottsdale because we got a really low rate at a great hotel there. It was worth the extra driving necessary to drop and pick me up those next few days. Plus, Scottsdale is a beautiful area, and since our anniversary was approaching, we wanted to celebrate by staying at a nice hotel for a few days.

It was in Scottsdale that I began to "swim" in the outdoor pools after each day's run. By swimming, I mean sitting in the pool. At best, I dog paddle around a little. But just standing in the pool felt so good. I would usually have a tall cup of ice-cold Coke to sip on as I walked around inside the pool. It was so hot this time of year that the water was a perfect temperature. After about an hour, I'd get out and shower, feeling loose and relaxed.

Running through New Mexico, we found that most of the hotels had indoor pools. I think the consistent high winds had something to do with that. When we got to Globe, a small copper mining town east of Phoenix, I decided to swim after I ran. As soon as we got back to the hotel after that day's run, I put on my bathing suit and hopped into the pool. It was so refreshing and relaxing that from Globe, moving westward, I swam almost every day.

We got to Scottsdale on a Friday and I was looking forward to having Saturday off. It was also around this time that I began to sense the end in sight. I was about 300 miles from attaining my goal: the Pacific. I had 104 days down and about 15 to go. It was hard for me to believe. That dream I had over 20 years ago in Boston—barring anything unforeseen happening—was going to be my reality in about three weeks. But I didn't want to get too cocky at this point.

The daily, refreshing dips every afternoon were enjoyable. I felt good and I could begin to envision my splashdown in the Pacific.

Not only was the end in sight, but Sheryl got to spend time in a big city while I was running. She had about had it with strolling up and down the aisles at the local Walmart in the small towns along the way. She was also so done with the Dollar General stores in the really small towns. Chitchatting with the checkout girls was a good way to pass the time for her, but enough was enough. With stays at the Scottsdale hotel and the Wigwam resort just west of Phoenix for over a week, Sheryl had the pleasurable break she needed and deserved. This must have been the vacation part of the trip Jeffrey referred to when he said, "This run will be the best vacation of your life."

We were fortunate to be in this locale to celebrate the Fourth of July and our anniversary on the fifth. Although it wasn't at the level of our 30th anniversary celebration in the South Pacific, it was still a great way to celebrate our 40th, an event we will never forget.

We were told that the Fourth of July celebration near Arizona State University in Tempe, called Tempe Town Park, was the place to be. So, on the Fourth and fifth, I decided to skip my run and just enjoy the two-day break and actually make a vacation out of the time.

UNFORGETTABLE FOURTH OF JULY IN TEMPE TOWN PARK IN TEMPE, ARIZONA.

On the Fourth we spent the afternoon in Scottsdale's Old Town, a district that resembled the Old West, with shops and restaurants. We walked around in the 114-degree heat checking out the area and ended up at a bar. We lucked out because they were having an outdoor barbeque, and the deal was, if you buy a beer, the hamburgers and hotdogs from the grill were free.

This was also our first experience with mist sprayers. As we sat outside in the scorching heat having cold beer, hotdogs, and hamburgers, we were cooled off by a fine mist coming from the overhang on the patio. It turned out to be a great way to spend the afternoon before we headed over to Tempe to see ASU and enjoy the Fourth of July celebration.

When we got to the river area, it was just beginning to get crowded. We were there early so we took our time to familiarize ourselves with the river neighborhood and the stadium where the Fiesta Bowl is played. We maneuvered through the crowd and found a good vantage point from which to see the fireworks. We got some food and sat back to watch the throngs of people passing by. We saw a lot of tattoos parading before us. What a relaxing afternoon leading up to the fireworks display.

When it was dark, the fireworks began. This was, by far, the longest and best pyrotechnic display we had ever seen. It lasted 53 minutes. From what we could see as we exited, they were shooting the fireworks from a boat or a bridge. They were magnificent. We began our trek back to the parking lot during the big finale so we could get a head start on the traffic that would be leaving. It still ended up taking over an hour to get out of the parking lot.

What a great way to celebrate the Fourth: beer, hotdogs, hamburgers, 114-degree heat, fireworks by the river, and running across America. A Fourth we'll never forget!

40TH ANNIVERSARY DINNER—ROKA AKOR
SCOTTSDALE, ARIZONA—JULY 5, 2011.

The next day was our 40th anniversary. Since I didn't run, we slept late and just toured the city. That night we decided to try an unusual Japanese restaurant named Roka Akor. After an amazing dinner and a dessert presented to us by the staff to celebrate our milestone, we were entertained by a freak dust storm outside the restaurant. The winds were blowing at 60 miles an hour. The waiters had to put chairs against the doors to keep them from flying open.

We stood there watching trees bend as the wind spread red dust over everything. When it finally passed, we walked outside to find all the cars in the parking lot covered in red dust. We had no idea where our car was. Every car was the same color. Fortunately, license plates were not completely covered in dust so we looked for a car with a Georgia license plate and finally found it.

The next day in the hotel's parking lot we saw trees down and red-dusted cars everywhere. The dust storm must have had an effect on the temperature because I ran that day in only 103 degrees. That was the lowest temperature I'd experienced in weeks. It was very comfortable by comparison.

Our days in Phoenix and Scottsdale will always be those of good memories of the Fourth of July celebration and our 40th anniversary. Even better days followed at The Wigwam.

CHAPTER THIRTY-FOUR

The Wigwam Resort— Oasis in the Desert

We were on a strict budget and so the majority of the motels we stayed in along the way weren't what we were used to, but they were necessary evils on our trip. In a lot of the areas out west—and by west, I mean west of Lubbock, Texas—these motels were all that were available. Even if money was no object, we'd still have no other choice in some of the very secluded and isolated areas we went through.

We stayed in Scottsdale before we entered the desolate region of west Arizona where roads and motels were a scarcity.

Sheryl, our CEO of accommodations, used the Internet to look for lodging possibilities in this sparsely populated part of Arizona. She came across a place called The Wigwam. The rates were so reasonable that she exclaimed aloud that there had to be a mistake; this beautiful resort had Internet rates of $79 per night. I suggested she call the resort to check it out.

When Sheryl called, she discovered that during the summer, Phoenix is so hot that tourists don't go there and even the locals usually spend as much time as possible in the cooler climate of the mountains to the north.

The posted rates were correct. We would be able to stay at a beautiful golf and tennis resort that was listed in the National Historic Registry of Hotels for $79 a night. We were used to much less sumptuous Days Inns and Motel 6s for $99 a night. For a few days, it looked like we would be in heaven. The pictures on the Internet were beautiful and the description of the resort's beginnings gave the impression that The Wigwam was first-rate with a lot of history behind it.

The day of our proposed first night at the resort, I ran down Camelback Road to my rendezvous point with Sheryl, Litchfield Park. As it turned out the resort was only five minutes away.

We checked in and, in the course of registering, Sheryl mentioned what we were doing. We got our keys and went to our room. This was not a room; it was an adobe casita, a bungalow, furnished in a western style and with modern amenities. I thumbed through the resort guest book and discovered there were two swimming pools, a few restaurants, three golf courses, tennis courts, a library, and conference rooms.

THE WIGWAM RESORT—A WELCOME RELIEF IN THE DESERT.

The resort started as a getaway for executives from Goodyear Tire and Rubber Company during the cold winter months in the Midwest. There was a small building that accommodated the meetings. From this humble beginning, it grew into a resort for the executives and their families and eventually was opened to the public. Goodyear selected the area to grow a special species of cotton (used in tires, according to resort personnel) for their products, thus the neighboring town, Goodyear.

When the staff learned what we were doing, they sent us a huge welcome basket. They really treated us well. We originally planned to stay only two nights but, because of our welcoming hosts and luxurious accommodations, and the fact there was a severe scarcity of hotels between Phoenix and the California border, we decided to stay an additional four nights. We would drive the extra distances each day for my runs.

To stay at the Wigwam was well worth the extra driving. Our other choice would have been to stay in Blythe, California, and drive east for each day's run.

Every day after my run, Sheryl and I returned to the Wigwam and went swimming. The pool was big and beautiful and almost always empty. Summer temperatures ranged, on average, between 105 and 115 degrees, and people didn't flock to Arizona desert resorts at this time of year. We felt like we had a 400-acre, magnificent oasis all to ourselves. We'd sit in the pool for hours and have a casual dinner in the evening.

This was a wonderful vacation and the best part of the run. We had a total of six terrific nights at the resort while I ran in the absolute worst heat of the day. And now I was mere weeks from the end of my run. It was here that I began to get really excited about reaching the Pacific Ocean and hugging Julie.

CHAPTER  THIRTY-FIVE

Dips in the Road
Southern California

Once I entered California, I was really feeling good. We were close enough (about 200 miles) to visit Julie and surprise her at her job. I could feel the end coming soon, and I decided to take in all I could before I finished in San Diego.

I needed help to navigate from Blythe, California, to the ocean because there are no straight east-west roads from the eastern border of California to the coast in San Diego. Also, no matter how I maneuvered, I knew I had to cross over the mountains to get to the coast.

THE DIPS IN SOUTHERN CALIFORNIA BETWEEN RIPLEY AND GLAMIS—WORST DAY OF THE RUN!

Larry, a friend of my cousins and a life-long resident of Southern California, went over the route with me via phone while I was in Phoenix. It was simple; take Route 78 to the outskirts of San Diego and then surface streets to wherever you want to finish.

Although the directions were straightforward, Route 78 was not. If you look at the map, Route 78 out of Blythe goes through farmland heading south, then west, then south, then west, then south. After over 2,000 miles of heading west, with only 200 miles to go, I had to start zigzagging. At least the first 60 miles of Route 78 were flat as a pancake and through very pretty farmland. That is, until I hit "The Dips."

The Dips, as the signs say, are steep ups and downs along a stretch of road between Ripley and Glamis, where the Imperial Sand Dunes are. Here are the problems with The Dips: First, there are no shoulders to run on as a safety factor. Second, as cars approach, they are not visible until they peak the top of the hump and are already on top of you. When you are running up the dips approaching the top, a car suddenly appears only a few feet in front of you.

After a while, I decided for safety's sake, to run/walk in the desert alongside the road. I had to pay close attention while I was running this stretch and it wasn't fun. But I opted for safety, even if I had to run through dirt.

Toward the end of this stretch, and toward the end of my 20 miles for the day, I started feeling bad. I was at the end of my fluid mixture and it was another scorcher, about 114 degrees. On top of that, there was no cell service. I tried to call Sheryl to pick me up a little early, but I couldn't reach her. I started feeling really weak and lightheaded. I was on a road with no shoulder, and I started to feel like I was going to pass out. I managed to climb up the embankment just as I blacked out.

I lay in the dirt for a few seconds, I believe. My heart was pounding as I lay there with my eyes closed. I was thinking about an old Western I had seen as a teenager. A cowboy was in the desert with no water. He was in the burning sun and his lips started to crack from the heat and dryness. He finally passed out.

I couldn't remember any of the details, I just knew I was in the desert with no water, and I had to wait until Sheryl came at the five-hour mark. I was disoriented so I didn't move for a few minutes. All I cared about was that I was off the road and safe, lying in the dirt. I didn't want to take a chance trying to get up just yet and collapse onto the road.

I was out of fluids so all I could do was wait for Sheryl to come along. I didn't want her to see me lying in the dirt, so I finally sat up and then gradually got on my feet and stood there. I looked at my watch and figured that if she was on time I had to wait only another 10 minutes. If she got lost or had car trouble, I would be screwed. My heart was racing, and I felt weaker than I had at the Tonopah exit.

When you feel this bad, time crawls. Finally, I saw her coming and I tried to look as if everything was normal. She had to stop about 50 yards past me because there was no shoulder to pull onto. I walked to the car and got in.

As soon as Sheryl saw me she knew I was in bad shape. I could barely talk. I said I'd be fine; I just needed something to drink. Sheryl handed me a Coke and a cup of ice, but it was impossible for me to pour the drink into the cup. She finally took it from me and poured. She started asking me questions about what was wrong, and I pleaded with her to let me just sit and drink. My breathing was very shallow. I'd never experienced this before.

The drive back to Blythe took about an hour. I sat like a limp noodle, taking shallow breathes and drinking occasionally. We traveled in silence until we passed Ripley, about 20 minutes from the hotel, and I finally felt better. By the time we got

HEADING UP THE MOUNTAIN TOWARD JULIAN, CALIFORNIA.

back to the hotel, I was feeling much better. I told Sheryl that was the worst I had ever felt. I didn't tell her I passed out until months after I finished the run.

When we got back to the room, I put my bathing suit on and went down to the pool to sit in the water. The hotel, a Comfort Inn, had a nice pool and, for the four days we were there, I used it every day. All I wanted to do was get in and just sit. The water was a perfect temperature and it felt great. After about 30 minutes I was back to normal and felt fine and began thinking ahead about the finish, only a week away.

Considering the number of miles I had run, I am amazed that I had only two very bad days of running. I had gotten so used to the minor annoyances and inconveniences along the way that I accepted it all as normal. I have to admit, I was surprised at my ability to handle the stress I was putting my body through and how I managed to recover so quickly. I never thought that any ills I experienced either of those two days were due to age. I don't think age was ever a factor in this entire endeavor. I think I would have felt poorly those two days, no matter how old I was.

CHAPTER  THIRTY-SIX

The Little Lady

If you recall the movie Private Benjamin starring Goldie Hawn, you remember a woman who had her world turned upside down, literally overnight, with the death of her husband on their wedding night. The comedy is about a woman who inadvertently joined the Army and, after fighting the system, realized that her only salvation was to accept and embrace her new life. Toward the end of the movie Private Benjamin not only endured, but thrived, grew, and embraced her new world, and became a much stronger, more contented woman.

I mention this movie because Sheryl was faced with losses almost overnight and was then asked to put her life on hold, to leave family and friends, to go on a cross-country journey with her husband, just so he could fulfill a 20 year-old dream, to run across the United States.

The experience of hopping from one cheap hotel to the next, loading and unloading luggage almost daily with each new hotel, finding and making reservations for hotels in obscure parts of the country, going to local coin-operated Laundromats to do laundry, and occupying hundreds of hours visiting Dollar General stores and talking to the checkout girls in tiny towns across the country, was Sheryl's new world for 5½ months. Not knowing what the future would hold and our living out of a suitcase were not what she envisioned for her sixtieth year of life.

She made only three demands of me at the outset: First, we would never camp out. We had to have a roof over our head every night. Second, we could not go near the Mexican border—very unsafe. And third, she had to bring her own toilet paper.

There is no woman I know who would have ultimately embraced this run with as much enthusiasm as Sheryl when the initial shock wore off. After the realization of our losses, and after Jeffrey's description of this new, wonderful vacation on the horizon, and after the flow of tears and loss of hope, Sheryl put her faith in me and accepted this enormous challenge I was putting us through. In the face of unemployment, losing the house, very little money, and a much unknown future, Sheryl was able to accept and embrace my simple approach of taking one day at a time, and to view our journey as an opportunity to see life from a different vantage point.

When I first started my run in February in Florida, I heard a professional runner was starting his transcontinental run from Los Angeles to New York, running 40 to 50 miles a day. The difference in our runs, besides the fact that he was a professional and was going to run farther each day, was that he had a support staff and a large caravan that he travelled with. He had a nutritionist, chef, fellow runners, a camera crew, and other personnel.

THE END OF A DAY'S RUN. SHERYL WAITING TO PICK ME UP. TIME TO EAT!

When I heard about this runner's effort, I was impressed that he was able to get media exposure, not only from the Regis and Kelly morning show, but from the President and First Lady. I think he was running to promote health and good nutrition for our nation's kids. He brought politically correct attention to the huge problem of obesity in our country.

Sheryl and I laughed as we drew quick comparisons of our two runs across America. He had a big RV to travel and sleep in. We stayed in cheap hotels and crammed our belongings into a small, 11-year-old sedan. He had a full staff of trained personnel. I had Sheryl. I ran 20 miles a day at a very relaxed pace and took pictures with my cell phone. According to reports, he ran 40 to 50 miles every day, over a 12-14 hour period. He ate 10,000 calories of healthy food prepared by a chef. I ate 4,000 calories, mostly sandwiches, hamburgers, hotdogs, French fries, and potato salad from Walmart, or fast-food for lunch and dinner, or at buffets and cheap restaurants. He wore the latest in running fashion and technology. I ran in the same clothes I had run in for the past 20 years. He had plenty of national media coverage. I had a few TV interviews and some news articles. He was skinny as a rail, a typical ultra-marathoner's physique. I had more meat on my bones. I lost no weight on the run.

He was on a mission. I was on a journey. I wouldn't have traded places with him for anything.

Sheryl was having so much fun and really doing everything she could to make sure I did, in fact, make it to the Pacific, that I decided as I ran into Mississippi, that I was not going to say or do anything to dampen her spirits or have her feel that I would not finish the run. Every day when she picked me up, she'd ask, "How was it?" No matter how bad the run, no matter how hot and tired I was, I always answered, "It was great!"

I DON'T WANT TO HEAR ABOUT OVERPOPULATION. THERE'S PLENTY OF ROOM. QUIT BUNCHING UP!

There were a few exceptions in the heat of the west, but by then I had assured Sheryl that there was no way I was not going to finish this run. If I had to crawl or finish in a wheel chair or on crutches, I was going to make it to the Pacific Ocean and hug Julie. She believed me, and I was able to let her in on my few bad days towards the end.

Sheryl and I laughed at the absurdity of our predicament and discussed route changes, fear of auto breakdown, fire and smoke, food to eat, and minor injuries.

The one thing I could not discuss with her was directions. I realized after only a few days running in Florida, that Sheryl was missing the compass gene altogether. No matter the obvious markers, Sheryl could not get directions right. I knew she had a bad sense of direction, but since I usually drove when we were together, it was never an issue. But now, since Sheryl had to pick me up every day, driving 5 to almost 80 miles in unknown territory, she had to figure it out herself.

I finally told her, "Just remember I am always running west, never east." I realized that no matter what I said, no matter how detailed the explanation, Sheryl could not navigate. I resigned myself to simply telling her to turn either right or left out of the motel parking lot and always reminding her that the sun comes up behind us in the mornings and we are running or driving toward the sun in the afternoons.

We bought two compasses to put on the dashboard. For some bizarre reason, they would not point west. We finally threw them away. I had to laugh at our situation and wound up giving her the nickname, "Maggie Magellan."

I did find it hard to laugh once when I found myself standing in the middle of

A DIRT ROAD IS SAFER THAN NO-SHOULDER HIGHWAYS.

the desert waiting to be picked up, and 20 minutes later Sheryl pulled up and told me she headed east for a while. I'm just grateful she realized she needed to turn around.

During the run, I went through periods where I craved a certain food or drink and then, after a week or so, became sick of it. This was no big deal except that Sheryl, in an effort to keep my food and liquid intake at a healthy level, would go out and buy a week's supply of whatever it was I longed for.

At the beginning of our trip, I drank large quantities of Gatorade. Sheryl worked to make sure I was properly hydrated and do it economically, so she got cases of orange Gatorade. A few days later, I became disgusted with the taste of orange Gatorade. I couldn't force myself to drink it. So we were stuck with two cases of orange Gatorade. I felt bad, but I couldn't take another swig of that stuff. We were stuck with the cases. I switched to the blue Gatorade and was fine. Sheryl went out and got two cases of the blue Gatorade. Even though I felt bad for Sheryl, after a week, I was sick of blue, too. Sheryl had to juggle so many conflicting circumstances.

For 5½ months we were together every day for at least 19 hours. During that entire time, we had only two disagreements. I remember thinking toward the end of the run that it was amazing that we had gotten upset with each other on only two occasions. The two of us lived, ate, slept, talked, and laughed together, mostly by ourselves, for almost 170 straight days. What a great time we had!

Under no circumstances could I have run 2350 miles and had so much fun without Sheryl. We were a two-man team.

Kudos to Sheryl and thanks to her for believing in me and following my dream with me.

CHAPTER ❸❼ THIRTY-SEVEN

Splashdown in the Pacific

My cousin Brian has a neighbor, Myrna, in public relations. For fun, she decided to make a few contacts with the local TV station to see if they were interested in covering my final day's run to the Pacific.

SHERYL, READY TO GO EVERY MORNING, PREPARING TO DROP ME OFF IN POWAY FOR THE 20-MILE RUN INTO SAN DIEGO.

Two local San Diego stations jumped on it. My final run was to be shot live on the six o'clock morning news. In order to do this, I had to get up at 4 a.m. that Thursday morning and be at the place I had ended the day before by 5:30 a.m. to run the final 2.3 miles and meet Julie. She had my flags, and we would finish together in front of the cameras, as the station requested.

I went to bed early that Wednesday night but was awakened by my son and granddaughter who flew in from Atlanta to surprise us. I was shocked as Sheryl opened the door and Jason and Rachel walked in. Rachel ran over to me and gave me a hug. I got up and hugged Jason. I couldn't believe they had flown in to be with me at the end. It was past 10 p.m., but we talked for a while before I tried to go back to sleep. Surprisingly, I did sleep and woke up at four when the alarm went off. From day one, I never used an alarm clock to wake up to run, but I was on a schedule that morning.

The first thing I did was call Jeffrey on Skype. He was in Israel, six hours ahead. He had been the first person I told about my plan back in January, and I wanted to thank him for all his help on that final morning. He was as excited as I was, so I felt he was with me.

The plan was for Sheryl to drive me to the spot where I stopped the day before on my final 20-mile run. That left me with 2.3 miles to go on the final day. I was to meet Julie about two blocks from the Crystal Pier where the cameras were set up to film live for the six o'clock morning news.

Sheryl dropped me off at the gas station on Grand Ave. I hadn't even considered that I would be running in darkness. As I began my quick run to meet Julie, I was trying to enjoy the final moments, but at the same time, trying to see where I was going. There were no lights so I had to run carefully so as not to misstep and end with an injury.

FINAL DAY, JULIE RAN WITH ME TO THE PACIFIC.

Fortunately, as I ran, the sun began to creep up, and as I approached Julie, I was finally able to see my way. I was pumped and excited, despite my having to watch every step; I was very early when I got to Julie. She was standing at the corner of Fanuel Street and Grand Avenue—apropos since we had lived in Boston for 14 years and visited Faneuil Hall many times. She had my flags and was ready for our short jaunt to the pier. I gave her a big hug and just held her, realizing that this moment, although not standing in the Pacific, was what I had dreamed about for five and a half months. Hundreds of times during the longest run of my life, I would think about seeing Julie's beautiful smile at the end of my run. It was exactly as I had imagined. I just held Julie and closed my eyes for a few seconds to savor this long-awaited moment.

PICKING JULIE UP 2 BLOCKS AWAY FROM PACIFIC BEACH. FLAGS IN HAND. READY TO FINISH.

I had decided somewhere in western Arizona that I wanted to carry three flags with me to the finish: The Israeli flag, the American flag, and the University of Alabama Crimson Tide flag. I debated the order I should place the flags. I knew how they were supposed to be placed but decided to put the Israeli flag above the U.S. flag with the Alabama flag at the bottom. I had put some thought into this because I certainly had the time while running and I wanted to make my own statement. It wasn't like I expected to have thousands waiting at the pier cheering my run into the Pacific. In fact, I expected only Sheryl, Julie, and my cousins. I was doing this for me, and I wanted to feel that I was showing my pride in being Jewish and be able to, in a very small but meaningful way, show my support for Israel, a small country that seems to attract fear and hatred from around the world. I wanted whoever would be watching to know that I was an American Jew, not a Jewish American. I was proud of my homeland in the face of world condemnation. It was a small statement that spoke volumes about how I felt.

I had been instructed to call Mark, from the PR firm when I reached Julie, and we met him at the corner. He was coordinating my final run, with the camera crew at Crystal Pier. Julie and I headed toward Pacific Beach. We talked and laughed as we ran the final few hundred yards of my 2350 miles. It was surreal that I was, indeed, at the end and I had, indeed, run across the United States from the Atlantic Ocean to the Pacific Ocean. I was so happy and excited. I had a flashback to my first marathon and how I felt as I crossed the finish line.

We stopped at the entrance to the Pacific Beach area, expecting to see Mark and the camera crew. Julie and I saw no one. I called Mark again and he said everyone was at the Pier, which was one block north of where we were.

Julie and I ran to the next block and there he was, along with the camera crew and reporter, Mike Castellucci. We were told that it would be just a few minutes before we went live for the 6:15 a.m. segment of the Morning Show. As I stood there with Julie and Mark, I was laughing to myself that after 2350 miles, I had to wait to run the last few yards through the sand to the water. It was a technical TV thing.

I just stood there and shook my head and smiled. After 118 days, my final 100-yards was being choreographed for the TV cameras.

As Julie and I were waiting for the newscast to begin, a man riding a bike stopped to speak to us. He asked me if I knew that the American flag always flies on top of any other flag. I told him that Israel needs my support a lot more than the United States does these days. He replied, "Then why didn't you run across Israel?"

Julie began to move away fearing a confrontation. I told him running across the width of Israel, anywhere from 7 to 85 miles depending on where you were in the country, wouldn't have been a challenge. It would have taken approximately four days at most. He looked at me and rode away.

Mike gave the signal for Julie and me to run to the pier as the cameras rolled and the reporter told my story on air. There were three separate segments to the interview; the last piece they filmed Julie and me going down the steps to the beach and running to the water.

I passed well-wishers and family—Sheryl, Jason, Rachel, my cousins, and some of their friends. They were holding up signs congratulating me as I passed. When I got to the water I looked at my shoes as the waves splashed over them. That was the moment that completed my run. It was over. I felt like Robert Redford in the 1972 movie, The Candidate, when he had won the election and just sat on the side of his bed and said, "Now what do I do?"

I stood there for a moment and for a split second returned to my start at the Atlantic, remembering stepping into the water and running through the sand toward the road to begin my run. And here I was across the country.

I turned to face the cameras and began to wave my flags. This was my victory lap. I felt like I was on top of Everest and had conquered the world. It was the Super

Bowl victory, The World Series seventh-game win, The BCS Championship, and Wimbledon, all wrapped up in one.

I had won the challenge. There were no other competitors or teams or participants to beat. It was just me and what I had at my disposal to accomplish what I did.

As I walked away from the water, I looked up and standing there smiling were my brother-in-law and sister-in-law, Nessim and Diane. Sheryl had been planning with them to be there at the end. I had no idea. They were at the foot of the steps, hidden behind a huge sign of congratulations. There they were, like a true brother and sister, sharing the moment with us. They had flown in the day before from New York and were staying in the hotel without my knowledge. Not just in-laws, but my dear friends.

MY SIX-MONTH MOTIVATION WAS TO HUG JULIE AS WE STOOD IN THE PACIFIC OCEAN.

With the shock of seeing Diane and Nessim, I felt a surge of emotion wash over me. I hugged them both, and it hit me. I turned away from the crowd, put my hands over my face and cried. I was so overwhelmed with what I had just completed and, at the same time, feeling a sense of loss for what I would no longer experience.

For those few moments I didn't know what to do with myself. I was lost. And then it was over. I wiped my face, turned, and walked back to the gathering.

Jason, Rachel, Nessim, and Diane, flew in to share the event with Sheryl, Julie, Brian, Susan, and me. What an incredible ending to the adventure of a lifetime. My sister-in-law, Suzie, had planned from day one to be there with us, but my finish being so close to the Sabbath on Friday, kept her from flying in.

MY BROTHER-IN-LAW, NESSIM, AND MY GRANDDAUGHTER, RACHEL, SURPRISED ME BY FLYING IN TO SEE ME FINISH. THEIR WELCOME SIGN.

My cousins, Brian and Susan, who live in San Diego, were there to video record the end. They were gracious enough to wake up very early, drive to Crystal Pier, and be there for the final moments. I hadn't seen Brian in 15 years. We used to play stick ball on family trips to Brooklyn as kids. It was great to reconnect.

COUSIN BRIAN AND ME IN SAN DIEGO. HE AND WIFE SUSAN WERE FIRST-CLASS HOSTS AS WE ENDED OUR RUN.

That afternoon, another TV station came out to the hotel to interview me for the evening news. The interviewer was very nice and did a more in-depth interview with Sheryl and me. He filmed all of us relaxing around the pool and encouraged Sheryl and me to discuss the run. He even recorded Rachel holding the mic up to me and asking a few questions. It was fun, and the piece came out great. We didn't see it when it was aired, but the interviewer made a recording of it and I was able to pick it up at the station.

The next day, as we were sitting by the pool, a team of teenage baseball players and their parents were lounging around as well. When I got up to go to the restroom, one of the parents stopped me and asked if I was the guy who just ran across the country. I told him I was, and he got excited and yelled to the kids to come over and get their picture taken with me.

MY BROTHER-IN-LAW AND SISTER-IN-LAW FLEW IN FROM NEW YORK TO BE WITH ME AS I TOUCHED THE PACIFIC OCEAN.

The kids jumped out of the pool and gathered around me as the parents lined up to take the group pictures. The boys jumped back in the pool after the photo op and the parents asked questions about my run. I felt a bit embarrassed but enjoyed talking to the parents and answering their questions.

I shook their hands and thanked them. I then realized that this was all great and fun, but I knew the little attention I was getting would last only for a fleeting moment. I decided to enjoy it. I knew that in a day or two the world would move on and I would slide back into anonymity where I belong, and feel comfortable.

My run was my run.

CHAPTER  THIRTY-EIGHT

The End of the Road

NEXT TO THE LAST DAY. LAST 20-MILE DAY BEFORE HEADING FOR CRYSTAL PIER.

If you have fulfilled a 20-year dream, what does it feel like as the journey comes to an end? Fortunately, on a cross-country run you're able to revel in the final hours as you head to the finish line. I had planned the final two days so that I could have one final easy 20-mile run through the suburbs of San Diego. I reflected on the past 5½ months and was able to enjoy the memories. I saved the final two miles for the last day to give me time to reflect and remember.

I found it hard to believe—surreal, in fact—that I had actually run across our country. I had no major injuries, no accidents, nothing but the best adventure of my life, and it was coming to an end. Each day for 118 days, I put on my running clothes, greased my feet with Vaseline, ran Glide on my inner thighs, smeared sunscreen on my face, put on my hat and sunglasses, and made sure my phone was charged. I put money, a small weapon, and mace in my pouch, gave Sheryl a kiss, and off I'd go. One hundred and eighteen days.

My job was to run. Just run. Over 5,700,000 steps. 144 nights in hotel/motels. 19 different hotel chains. 47 different hotel and motel rooms. 472,000 calories consumed. 8 pairs of running shoes. 48 pairs of socks. 8 jars of Vaseline. 6 short sleeve T-shirts. 7 long sleeve T-shirts. 2 hats. 2 pairs of shorts. Over 1,200 pictures and videos. 119 daily blogs on my web site. Gallons of Coke, Gatorade, Ruby Red, ice tea, cold water, warm water, nasty water. 56 packs of Berries and Cherries. 86 Fig Newton bars. 272 towns and cities. One wedding. One funeral. One birthday. A support staff of one. Passover. A 60th birthday. A 40th wedding anniversary. 16,000 miles driving in order to run 2350 miles. Oh, and 592 gallons of gas.

As I was training at the YMCA in Marietta, before telling anyone what I was planning to do, I began thinking of what it would be like to run across the entire United States, from coast to coast. My biggest concern was injuries. At any time during the run, I could have had a run-ending injury or accident; pulled or torn muscles, foot problems, leg injuries, or auto accidents, or just called it quits.

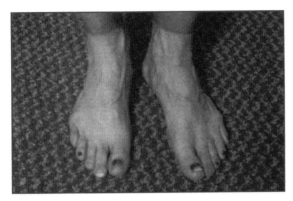

DIRTY LEGS AND BLACK TOENAILS PLAGUED ME EVERY DAY OF THE TRIP.

There had to have been luck attached to my run. The fact that I had no accidents and only minor physical ailments, other than my lower leg, was miraculous. I ran virtually trouble free for 119 days. In fact, I have run over 7,500 miles over the past 22 years with no major injury. This is unheard of in the world of running.

While running, I have always been aware of what was happening with my body. I could sense when something serious was wrong and when something could be ignored. I always considered any illness, injury, or physical discomfort as a minor annoyance that would pass.

If I ever felt something was serious, I'd attend to it and then move on. That knot on my lower leg in Mississippi was a mystery to me. I haven't asked a doctor what it could have been. It doesn't matter. All I know is that it was so painful I had to miss one day of running. By continuing to run and, with a brief visit to the acupuncturist, the pain gradually disappeared. I still have a slight bump where my left leg attaches to my foot.

COULD NOT HAVE PICKED A BETTER CITY TO RUN TO. SAN DIEGO, CALIFORNIA: PARADISE!

My toe nails have all grown back and are healthy again. My leg muscles are not as pronounced and well defined as they were during the run. I'm still wearing the last pair of shoes I wore as I stepped into the Pacific. I won't throw away any of my shirts from the trip, but I don't wear them either. I'll just keep them. Most of the shoes I wore were discarded along the way. There was no room in

211

the car to keep them around. I don't wear a hat or sunglasses anymore. I have to watch what I eat. I still run, but it's back to an hour and six miles, three to four times a week.

My priorities have changed. I have a hard time taking very many things seriously. What was important before seems less important now. When I'm alone, I return to somewhere on the road. The memories are still as crystal clear as when I ran. The wind. The hills. Fire. Smoke. Pies. VLA. Mountains. Rivers. Dry river beds. Snakes. Deer. Road kill. Police. Road crews. The sun. The heat. Bad hotels. Great hotels. The nice people. The homeless guys. The cars and trucks. Deserts. Dust devils. Sand dunes. Horses. Cows. Lone Stars. Bridges. The turtle that peed on me when I lifted him out of the road. Town squares. Convenience stores. Churches. The funeral home. Alan. Mary. Dickie. The Rabbi. The synagogue. Shabbat dinners. Swollen ankles. Salt on my face. Firemen. Wind Turbines. Wide open nothingness. Good flashbacks, all of them, all of the time.

That remaining knot on my lower leg still hurts a little when I push on it. I hope it stays there as a reminder.

The absolute best experience of my life.

C

Conclusion
Comments from Friends
and Strangers

Throughout my run, friends, family, and total strangers sent me encouraging words. Apparently what I was doing served as inspiration for many, something that caught me by surprise. Sometimes, as a little pick-me-up, I would use these kind words from others to help myself. If I was serving as inspiration for even one person, known or unknown, I felt a need to complete the run for that person as well as for myself.

I also came to realize that there were some who were vicariously living their dream of traveling through my run. This was both expressed and implied by many. All of the following and many more served as an incentive to continue my blog and make my entries as colorful, descriptive, and interesting as possible.

The following are only a few of the comments and remarks sent to me during the run.

- *Alan, Feb 17*

  This is a fantastic thing to do. We will follow your run with interest and spread the word. Have a great run.

- *Peppy, Feb 18*

  I don't know you, Richard, but I received this information from Corrine in Montgomery who is married to Larry (a cousin of mine through marriage). Mazel Tov on this unbelievable journey....I wish you good health and safety during your run across the USA.

- *Jim, Feb 19*

  Best of luck, Richard. Good to see you're keeping up the good fight.

- *Corinne, Feb 19*

  Run, Richard, Run!!! *We are so proud of you!! Who needs a GPS when you've got Sheryl!! Love you both.*

- *Eric, Feb 19*

  Best wishes, Richard, through your challenging journey. I support your efforts and the cause it represents. Stay safe and keep hydrated.

- *Gary, Feb, 20*

  This is a pretty amazing thing you are doing. I'm in awe. I've read everything on the web site, looked at all the clips and told lots of friends about it. Good luck. I'll check in regularly. See you at Gina's wedding. I've got lots of questions but I'll spread them out over time.

- *Robert, Feb 21*

  Best of luck on this amazing trip. Say hello to Brian when you get there.

- *Mark and Suzy, Feb 23*

  Please tell us your daily routine: When do you get up in the morning; what do you do/eat to prepare for the run; how close does Sheryl follow; what do you do to wind down during the afternoon; what kind of motels do you stay at; etc.?

  We love reading the daily blogs.

- *Brian, Feb 25*

  Hi Richard, I was with Eric at the USA Baby in Las Vegas yesterday and I was asking about you and he showed me your site. I think this is awesome and wish you and Sheryl the best through your travels across the US. I especially want to wish you and your family my thoughts in regards to your dad. I'll be thinking of you and your family during these hard times and applaud you for your mission at hand. I will be following daily on your journey as you blog about your days accomplishments and wish you nothing but the best.

  Safe travels.

- *Jeffrey, Feb 27*

  So sorry to hear about your father . . . what a sweet man he was.

  I have been following your run; am in Jerusalem until tomorrow, visiting my daughter who is here for the year; just made a small donation to support your run (via PayPal); wanted to send it from here, in memory of your father, for the sake of the good karma, etc. I could not get the Nefesh B'Nefesh site to take my money, but we can try that again when I get back to Atlanta.

  Best to everyone, and I am sorry that I can't be with you for your father's funeral.

- *Elliot, March 3*

  Unfortunately you and I have the same story to tell. We had our store for 37 years and we had to close this past November also due to the economy. Now both my wife and I are unemployed looking for work in this great economy.

I just wanted to write you a note to say hello and tell you that it's great what you are doing. Keep up the run and keep getting the word out there. Unless it happens to you, people do not realize how devastating it is to lose your business, and unless you are in this situation you can't even imagine how it feels.

Good Luck

- ### Kay, March 4

  Our group is so behind you (we cannot run fast enough to be out front). All the old timers who know you buzz about the blogs... We are proud to have you as a friend and to be contributing such effort to get attention to the non-working men and women who wished that wasn't so for them... God Bless and run safely.

- ### Annie, March 4

  Are you running on the weekend? I will probably go into withdrawal without hearing from you guys.

  Now tell me, Richard, where are you getting GOOD BAGELS in the middle of God's country? I bet you have some sent in from the big city. Please do not tell me that you are eating some that come in a plastic bag. I laugh a lot when I have visions of you and Sheryl on the road having a good time. I wish I could do that myself.

  Stay well and be careful. How is the body feeling?

  Miss you guys.

- ### Alan, March 5

  Richard. Very interesting observations. Can't wait to hear what you find in Alabama, Mississippi, Louisiana, Texas, New Mexico, Arizona and California.

- ### Susan, March 9

  I've been following your blog...pretty amazing.

- ### Kay, March10

  Your blogs are such fun...the videos of historic Defuniak Springs make me want to rush right there (but that was a very pretty bldg. there) and I would have loved to have recorded your plea for Sheryl to come quickly to the porn shop...

  Do people stop and ask you why you are making this run? Do they contribute to one of the causes? Have radio or TV crews availed themselves of such a great story of one man (and one woman) making a difference? If I knew the cities where you would be traveling, I would give a few folks a jingle on the phone—it's such a great human interest story.

Just one bit of news—Kathy M fell and broke her femur. She just had foot surgery and was back in the hospital getting this nailed back up... Poor Gal. You might know this already as she is an avid watcher of www.20AT60.com.

Gonna run off to bed and read a bit more of Mark Twain's Autobiography... it's fascinating... He did not allow it to be published until he had been dead 100 years... Run well, run lightly, run safely and the same goes for your manager to drive safely and keep her safe too....

- **Bobby, March 14**

From one of your oldest friends from Bear, Cloverdale, etc..., Bob, AKA Bobby. James posted your adventure on Facebook, and I wanted to shoot you a line... what an awesome adventure. Proud of you!

- **Susan, March 14**

Richard, You are amazing!!! Keep running and posting pictures. I love reading about your run.

An aging Baby Boomer

- **Woody, March 14**

Mary M. called and told me about your adventure. I am so proud I know someone brave enough and in shape enough to attempt this. Good luck and count me in for a contribution.

- **Robert, March 16**

I am so proud of you! Keep up the good work! After 400 miles of running, you are 17 percent of the way there! Awesome! I love reading your posts. Keep up the good work.

- **Gary, March 17**

Kudos on the 400 miles. Wow your run sounds a little "Easy Rider"-ish. Maybe when you're all done you can make a movie compiling all your pix and clips and call it Easy Runner.

BTW, the blue and orange Tiger reference was not immediately apparent to your northern cousins. But I Googled it. What did the world do before Google?

- **Kay, March 17**

We need to hear more about your nite in the small guest home... hope it didn't give you the creeps. Forgot to tell you about something that happened at our meeting last Thursday. Almost at the end, Jim G. was rustling about in a plastic bag. Someone was talking and people were listening... When I looked again he had a package of Fig Newtons and he passed them around for all to enjoy and think of our good friend Richard as we munched away... It was cool. I am now about to get into my car to head to the meeting... Tonite the other Sheryl is doing a program on meditation... Run well, run safe, and know we are thinking of you both.

- *Corrine, March 19*

  I love reading your posts every day!! Instead of majoring in psychology, you should have been journalism major—you have a wonderful way of writing and most days, I laugh!! Wishing you wonderful spring weather for many days—Keep feeling better and better!! Can't wait for Picnic Cafe in Dahlonega!

  Love you both!!!

- *Annie, March 19*

  I look forward to your posts every day. I am addicted to your photos and all the details of the people and towns. You guys are doing what a lot of people would like to do. The best way to see and feel a place is to get off the path and be part of the scenery.

  It will be very interesting when you get to Texas. I hope you strap on a set of horns and blend in with the locals. Every car/truck down there needs some attached to their hood.

  Take good care of yourselves and know we are back here enjoying your journey.

  Godspeed.

  Joe just waltzed by said hello and put up the Texas Horns gesture. Miss you all the time.

- *Corrine, March 20*

  Yeah for the 3rd state!! Watch out for the chickens and the trains- xoxoxo

- *Pattie, March 20*

  As native Mississippians, Jim and I hope that you'll experience genuine southern hospitality as you run through the state. Have a safe journey.

- *Ethan, March 21*

  This is Ethan. Sorry for the delay on this e-mail. Mom had mentioned to me that you had wanted to pass my name along to a web designer and I really appreciate the thoughtfulness! I have been pretty busy on my own, but thank you for thinking of me.

  I have been following your run and I am completely amazed! It is really a wonderful endeavor. I admire your drive and determination... I have been blown away with the idea of someone being able to run clear across the country since I saw Forrest Gump.

  I wanted to pass on a brief note. I am sure you are well researched, but I saw you are taking the I-10 route. I recently read that the stretch from Phoenix to San Diego is in a horrible state with the Mexican drug war. The article I read talked about abductions, gangs dressing up as police, and trained mercenaries taking surveillance positions. The agents quoted in the article said they have ceded all power in the area. I am sure some of it is political posturing, but PLEASE BE SAFE!!!

Looking forward to following the rest of your run!

All the best.

- **Jonah, March 22**

Renana from Nefesh B'Nefesh sent me this note about your run. Sounds amazing.

By my calculations, it sounds like you'll be getting to California sometime in June, and should be somewhere around the middle of the country around the beginning of May, right? Where is the middle of the country for you, exactly? And are there any Jewish spots along the way that you're stopping into? Where are you going to be for Passover?

I'll keep an eye on your Twitter feed and your Facebook wall—and maybe we can chat on the phone sometime in the coming weeks?

Best of luck.

- **Gary, March 24**

Thanks for the Biloxi Report. The Beach looks very nice. It's a comfort to know since we'll be vacationing there. What's this about a radio interview?

- **Annie, March 24**

Your stories are priceless and warming to my heart. I love hearing the tales of just one guy on the road and the response of the world around him. I feel good when I read your stories. I have a renewed faith in humanity. The people you are meeting and the places you see make one appreciate the world and life. I know they have as much fun with you as you with them. Laughter provides healing. That's why you can run 20 miles a day. The spirit of the people carries you. You are ready to meet the new list of characters tomorrow.

Nothing is new here on the plantation except tons of pollen and wonderful spring flowers. Always in my thoughts.

- **David, March 29**

I bet you were really glad to have someone to run with....after 500+ miles you finally found a friend. You need to try one of those snowballs, our favorite flavor is "cream ice cream" a little sweet but refreshing! Sue used to make fun of our snow cones with grape and cherry flavors. Louisiana snowballs r the best!

I have been logging a few more miles than normal...ran 9 Saturday and 6 Sunday just thinking of your 20 each day keeps me going.

Watching Bama play in the NIT shortly, hope you r tuned in. Be safe

- *Gloria, April 8*

  Enjoy reading your progress. Have fun!

- *Carlyn, April 15*

  I can't help but write you a personal note to show my support for your mission to create a wave of awareness throughout the nation! One of my best friends, Maxine Orange, from Montgomery, Ala, sent me your links. 20 miles a day, WOW, that is a lot!!! When do you plan to arrive in San Diego? I only ask because I will be back in SD June 9-15 and if that is your end time, I will 100% come out to support you! I was diagnosed with MS when I was 19... and at age 33, I ran 4 Half Marathons this year!! (NYC Half was my last a few weeks ago). I am fortunate since I have not had major symptoms since 2004... and since Tragedy Creates Purpose, I have discovered my love for running. As I like to say, "Move it or Lose it" :) But what you are doing is absolutely amazing.

  It's funny, after letting go of my life with Corporate America (aka, losing my job) on 11/11/10, I decided it was time for a change. So, on Jan 14, after selling all that I own that I considered stuff and shipping what was valuable, after living in California for 7 years, I left San Diego, Calif. and embarked on my six week Cross Country Road Trip (4849 miles— I did not go the "easy" route) to Wilmington, NC, where I have brought my California Unemployment Check (though the government has not paid me since 2/28 so I am in a new battle all together). Luckily the gas hike started as soon as my trip stopped.

  Now I am here, I'm paying the same in Rent as I am for my COBRA (but my rent is a lot less than Calif.). My case is different though. I am single, no kids, no house, paid car.... but at the same time, I am young with an uncertain future. Since NOTHING in life is secure, I've decided to take a new approach— Pursue My Passions. For the past 5 years I worked as a Nurse Recruiter (which I loved), but I can no longer count on helping others get jobs in this UNCERTAIN market. So, I have my blog below (which I'd love for you to read if you find yourself with downtime) and soon enough, hope to be Paid to be Me—and help others at the same time :)

  Anyhow, I simply want to wish you good luck, awesome running weather, lots of water and peaceful nights of sleep.

  Thanks for taking on this mission for ALL of us!

- *Shanna, April 18*

  I'm a friend of Ginger Boswell. She told me about you & your journey. I've posted your info on my Facebook page, hope that helps with donations. I was wondering what time you are leaving on Thursday and from where—and if you would like some company for a couple of miles? I'd like to run a mile or two with you if you are willing, but I understand if it's a solo journey.

- *Katie, May 18*

  Wow—best of luck to you and congratulations!!

- *Treon, May 24*

  I enjoyed sitting next to you on the plane to Memphis, so proud for both you and Sheryl for this undertaking. The bed and breakfast in Plains is the Rocking N and they can be contacted at 806-456-6877. Their website is http://www. newsomvineyards.com/bb.htm. Great place to stay with a lot of nice folks and history of West Texas. Hope you guys had a chance to eat at the Japanese food place on the corner of Quaker and 82nd called Hayashi. Enjoy! Praying for your run!

- *Mike, June 1*

  Tear 'em up Richard!

- *Corrine and Larry, July 12*

  Please be sure to eat enough- Don't scare us anymore-we worry about you!! xoxoox

- *Moshe, July 27*

  Thank you for all that you have given and will continue to give to so many other people, including myself, by your journey/adventure.

  I am so happy for you and Sheryl. I am especially thrilled that you did not experience any serious injury, at least nothing that halted your run.

  What an amazing accomplishment!

  MAZEL TOV!!

  G-d bless you and Sheryl always.

  Happy swimming!!!

Addendum

Sheryl and I, as we were on the run, gave our house back to the bank. I am currently engaged in small business consulting on a part-time basis. I have had numerous requests for interviews from various newspapers in the Southeast, and I have spoken a number of times at various business clubs about my experiences during the run.

We were fortunate to have raised quite a bit of money for the charities I ran for and for the run itself.

As I locked the door to our store and put a closed sign in the door, the feeling of sadness and relief hit me at once. The feeling of relief was expanded to a sense of freedom as I ran across the country. My drive to perform and achieve for 37 years has been replaced with the pleasures of sitting in a park or relaxing on a beach. My desire to drive myself, achieve, or even develop a new daily routine has been tempered.

Personally, as time passes, I discuss my run less and less with friends and family. It was a period of my life that I have set aside, publicly. Privately, though, not a day goes by that a memory or a flashback of a particular place or setting doesn't put a smile on my face or fill me with emotion.

Like that small knot on my leg that won't go away, my run is now part of me.